D0970839

Ecce Ancilla Domini

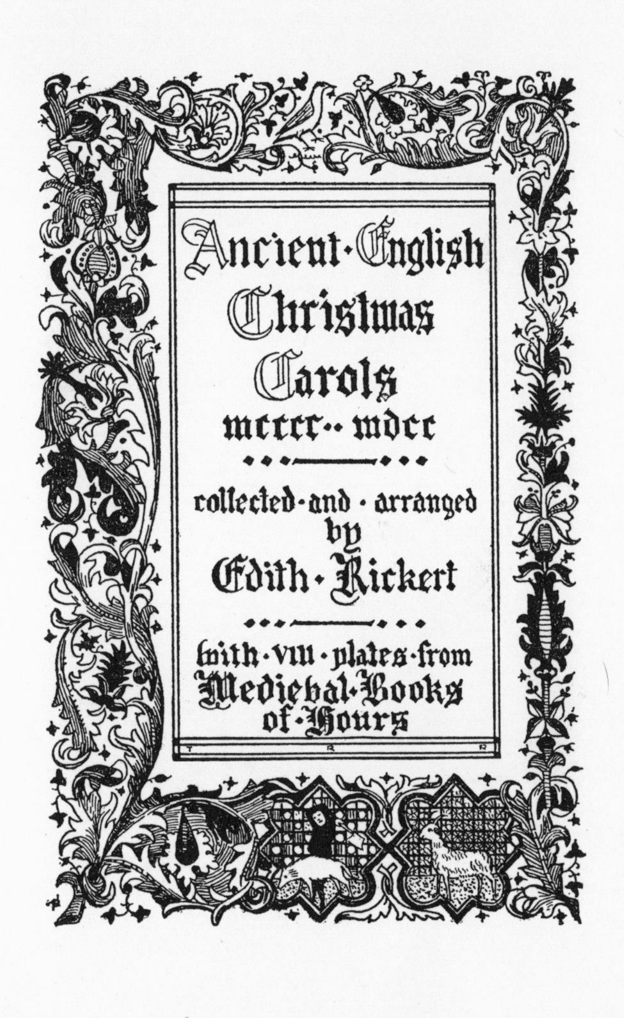

Ancient · English Christmas Carols

mcccc ·· mdcc

collected · and · arranged
by
Edith · Rickert

with · viii · plates · from
Medieval · Books
of · Hours

ANCIENT ENGLISH CHRISTMAS CAROLS MCCCC TO MDCC

COLLECTED & ARRANGED
BY EDITH RICKERT

COOPER SQUARE PUBLISHERS, INC.
NEW YORK
1966

Published 1966 by Cooper Square Publishers, Inc.
59 Fourth Avenue, New York, N. Y. 10003
Library of Congress Catalog Card No. 66-25700

Printed in the United States of America
by Noble Offset Printers, Inc., New York, N. Y. 10003

TO

E.Q.R. and F.E.R.

MY SISTERS

FOR WHOSE UNWEARIED ASSISTANCE

IN THE PREPARATION OF THIS LITTLE VOLUME

I AM DEEPLY GRATEFUL

The poems which appear on pages 3, 160, *and* 168 *were printed for the first time by Messrs. Chambers and Sidgwick in "Early English Lyrics," now issued by Messrs. Sidgwick and Jackson, Ltd.*

CONTENTS

PART I

CAROLS OF THE NATIVITY

PART II

CAROLS OF THE DIVINE MYSTERY

PART III

CAROLS OF YULETIDE FESTIVITY

ILLUSTRATIONS

INTRODUCTION

Antiquity of Carol Singing

"I pray you, sirs, both more and less,
Sing these carols in Christëmas."

So wrote John Awdlay, the blind and deaf chaplain of Haughmond Abbey in Shropshire, about the year 1426, showing that by this time the custom was well established in England. But indeed praise of "Dan Noël" can be traced back at least two centuries earlier. There is an Anglo-Norman carol, which was perhaps sung in the days of King John, in which Noël, after enjoining upon every man to keep open house and to furnish his neighbour drink "until he nods his head and sleeps by day," concludes with the old Saxon exchange of healths "Wesseyl" and "Drinc-heyl."[1]

This carol then suggests the probability that there were Yule songs, at least of the wassail type, among the Anglo-Saxons; and it is almost certain that customs originally pagan, such as the procession of the boar's head and the holly and ivy contests, would have been accompanied by some kind of song-dance.

[1] The carol is printed on p. 132.

The Word Carol

The word *carol*, whatever its origin,[1] is clearly associated at first with the idea of choric song. In French it is used regularly, as early as the beginning of the twelfth century, to describe the song-dance of spring and love that was in itself still almost a rite at that time.[2] In England the French word *carole* had been taken over before the beginning of the fourteenth century, and at first was used commonly in the secular sense; but by some freak in philology it came later to be applied almost entirely to Christmas songs, alike to those of a sacred character, such as in French have always been called *noëls*,[3] and to songs of revelry. Even as late as the seventeenth century, however, we find traces of its primitive significance, as in the title: *Clod's Carol, or a Proper New Jig.* But at the same period another title, *A Mournful Carol, or an Elegy*, &c., shows how loosely the term was used.

Origin of Sacred Carols

The history of carol singing is one phase of the struggle of the Church with the pagan instincts in man. Undoubtedly the feast of Yule[4]—the turn of the year at the winter

[1] French *carole*, according to Diez from Romance *corolar* or *coreiar* = *choreas ducere*; Jeanroy, from Greek *choraulein* = *to accompany with a flute*; Faidit, Latin *corolla* = *little ring*.

[2] *Aucassin and Nicolete* (§ 33, 1, 7), for example.

[3] From Latin *nātālem* = *birthday*.

[4] The origin of the word *Yule* is uncertain. It has been derived from various roots, including the Germanic *jehwela* = Latin *ioculus* = *mirth*; or the Germanic *jeula* = *snow-storm*.

solstice[1]—is of immemorial antiquity; and it was celebrated with a blending of riot and sacrifice to tribal divinities, such as is still found among barbaric races. Very early the Church issued a series of repressive decrees which indicate somewhat the character of the revels. In 408, stage plays were forbidden on the Lord's Day and other solemn festivals; in 425, on the Nativity and other Church feasts; in 578, disguisings were condemned on these occasions; in 614, "filthy plays" were prohibited on the Kalends of January.

With the era of St. Augustine, in England, came the policy of substitution in place of prohibition, and so gradually the theory was evolved: if the people must have plays for Christmas, let them be plays of divine mystery and miracle; if they must have songs, let them sing music of the Church.

How far this theory became explicit I do not know; it was certainly acted upon. The drama grew up within the Church, outgrew its bounds, and by a curious sort of compromise, when it reached the streets and market-places, took on much of the secular character that centuries before had led to decrees against it. Similarly, the carols that developed out of the Latin festival hymns, after they had grown somewhat away from their models, were presently found in the same manuscripts with songs of purely pagan origin.

The relationship of the early carols to the Latin hymns is unmistakable. They are at first macaronic, like the thirteenth century *Mater Salutaris*,[2] the Latin element

[1] In the *Saxon Chronicle*, as late as 1154, Christmas is called "midwintermas."

[2] P. 3.

being gradually reduced to a refrain and at last disappearing. The Latin phrases, which recur frequently, are all common in medieval hymnology. The verse is very often at first modelled upon the form of the hymns, in lines of four and three beats alternately. The sentiments of the early carols differ scarcely at all from those of the hymns. In all probability both were written by clerics, the carols representing an attempt, whether formulated or not, to bring the meaning of Christmas nearer home to the people.

It is to be noted that most of the great carol manuscripts belong to the fifteenth and sixteenth centuries; indeed, they may almost be said to be included between the reigns of Henry VI. and Henry VIII. There are, however, grounds for believing that some of the poems themselves go back to the days of Henry IV. and Richard II., possibly even of Edward III. This date would seem to show that carol writing was a part of the great fourteenth-century movement of the middle classes in England, of the stir towards democracy, of the conquest of the people's English over the Latin of the clergy, over the French of the court.

In this connection it is interesting to point out certain coincidences in theme and treatment which suggest that the carols and the mystery plays are but two phases of the same tendency towards the popularisation of religion. Not only were carols sung on the stage, as in the *Second Shepherds' Play* (Towneley Plays) and the *Pageant of the Shearmen and Tailors* (Coventry Plays), but the carols as a class are strongly dramatic, especially the Annunciation and Shepherd Carols and the lullabies; the last two groups indeed, in their realistic details and homely treatment, are strongly suggestive of scenes in the religious drama, to which they may owe their inspiration.

Pre-Reformation Carols

These are found almost entirely as collections, in less than a dozen great manuscripts which represent alike the taste of the court, the clergy, and the citizens. While the practice of carol-making undoubtedly arose among clerics, it soon spread widely among all classes of people, as is shown by the range of themes and treatment. Even the kings of this period fostered music: Henry VI. had a court musician famous over Europe, John Dunstable, who wrote carols;[1] Edward IV. was a great lover of pageantry; Henry VII. was a patron of musicians, and Henry VIII. himself was versed in song-making[2] and had a chapel full of composers, some of whom at least were probably their own poets.

Some day we may be able to identify to a much larger extent than at present the work of these court singers. Although names are often attached to the songs, we cannot be certain whether the attribution is for the words as well as for the music. When in 1504 William Cornish was paid for "setting of" a carol at Christmas, it would seem that

1 A fine manuscript in Trinity College, Cambridge (o.3. 58) is believed to contain thirteen carols of his composition. It was published by Fuller-Maitland and Rockstro, under the title *English Carols of the Fifteenth Century*, 1891.

2 MS. 31,922 in the British Museum, which contains various compositions by Henry VIII., has his name on the flyleaf, and is believed to have belonged to him.

he furnished the music only, although he is known to have been something of a writer. When two names are attached to one short lyric, as often happens in the case of Richard Smart (Smert) and John Truelove (Trouluffe), we know that they collaborated but cannot tell the share of each. And again, while we have a long list of names of composers [1] during the early part of the reign of Henry VIII., we can never be sure, in an age when authorship was rarely looked upon as a private right, how often the work is original and how often merely the setting, or possibly the adaptation of an old song, to music. For example, John Gwynneth, who is given credit for the Easter carol beginning, "And I mankind," was evidently adapting an old love-song, the refrain of which, "My love that mourneth for me," he retained. On the other hand, the composer Pygott, whose name is signed to the highly original song, "Quid petis, O Fili?" [2] in all probability wrote the words as well. The author of so unusual a poem, even in those days, would scarcely have been overlooked.

Aside from the court carols there are many of a more strictly ecclesiastical stamp, showing all degrees of poetic ability. They agree in a general tendency to interpret the great event in its relation to the soul of man; hence they often include a brief outline of the life of Christ and the Crucifixion. Some few are strongly mystical in character. The best are rather elaborate in structure and artificial in

[1] William and John Cornish, Banister, Sturges, Newark, Davy, Sheringham, Fairfax, Mower, Peter, Hawte, Pakke, and others.

[2] P. 63.

treatment, even extravagant, as, for example, "A blessed bird, as I you say."[1] The worst carols of this class are scarcely distinguishable from those of popular origin.

The usual mark of the carol made among the people and sung by them is its recurrence in several slightly different versions. Sometimes stanzas are added or omitted or displaced; sometimes the sense is confused by forgetfulness or misunderstanding or mishearing; sometimes whole lines or groups of lines are lost except their rhyme-schemes, which are then filled out, either to the same general purport, or with quite a different meaning.

All these changes are due to oral transmission extending over a considerable period of time. It is probable that some of the carols were gradually altered out of all resemblance to their original form; for instance, "Joseph was an Old Man," which in its present state cannot be older than the seventeenth century, is based upon a legend that was familiar in the fourteenth, and in the fifteenth was sung in a carol very similar in substance but totally different in structure and wording from the later version.[2] Again, the story of the eighteenth-century "Cherry-Tree Carol,"[3] is to be found in a fifteenth-century mystery play; while the fifteenth-century "The Falcon hath Borne my Make Away" has survived until to-day in a form singularly altered but quite recognisable.[4]

In content these popular carols are for the most part

[1] P. 186. It is perhaps better classified as an Easter carol.
[2] Cf. pp. 24–25, below.
[3] Cf. p. 88, and note on p. 153.
[4] Cf. pp. 193, 194.

religious; but they are more concerned with the story of the Nativity than with any subtleties of interpretation. Comparatively few of a secular type were written or have survived. These have to do with the immemorial customs of the revels in the hall, and include further a few wassail and drinking songs. Sometimes even in these the religious element was dragged in in a curious fashion, as when the boar was used as a symbol for Christ, or "Bring us in Good Ale," was sung to the tune of an Annunciation carol.

Post-Reformation Carols

The Reformation removed several of the chief sources of inspiration of the older carol-writers. It was no longer possible to sing "Regina celi, letare," or to turn rapturous love-songs, such as "Who shall have my Fair Lady?" or "True Love, you do me Right," to worship of the Virgin; or to glorify the Divine Motherhood with lullabies, unless these were understood to be spiritual Balulalows. There could be no more carols for saints' days, and even the Nativity itself had to be viewed less from a dramatic standpoint and more as a scheme of salvation. The religious elements were, so to speak, strained out from the popular accretions with which they had been mingled, consequently reduced as well as purified.

On the other hand, more stress than ever was laid on the old customs of Christmas mirth, and carols on this theme become increasingly numerous during the seventeenth century. Ben Jonson in "Christmas his Masque," presented at court in 1616, introduces a thoroughly secular "Carol, in a long tawny coat, with a red cap and a flute at his girdle, his torch-bearer carrying a song-book open; and Wassail, like a neat sempster and songster, her page bearing a brown bowl dressed with ribands and rosemary before her." Again, Nicholas Breton in his *Fantasticks* in 1626 gives a picture of Christmas revels in which the Christian element has become pretty well an appendix: "It is now Christmas, and not a cup of drink must pass without a carol; the beasts, fowl and fish come to a general execution, and the corn is ground to dust for the bakehouse and the pastry; cards and dice purge many a purse, and the youth show their agility in shoeing of the wild mare; now good cheer and welcome, and God be with you—and against the New Year provide for the presents—the Lord of Misrule is no mean man for his time, and the guests of the high table must lack no wine; the lusty bloods must look about them like men, and piping and dancing puts away much melancholy, stolen venison is sweet, and a fat coney is worth money, pitfalls are now set for small birds, and a woodcock hangs himself in a gin, a good fire heats all the house, and a full alms-basket makes the beggar's prayers: the maskers and the mummers make the merry sport, but if they lose their money their drum goes dead; swearers and swaggerers are sent away to the alehouse, and unruly wenches go in danger of judgment; musicians now make their instruments speak out, and a good song is worth the hearing. In sum, it is holy time, a duty in Christians in remembrance of Christ and customs among friends for the maintenance of good fellowship. In brief, I thus conclude it: I hold it a memory of the Heaven's love and the world's peace, the mirth of the honest, and the meeting of the friendly. Farewell."

This is the aspect of Christmas voiced chiefly in the popular carols of the late sixteenth and seventeenth centuries; it finds expression also in the work of the poets Herrick and Wither, and continues until the gradual spread of Puritanism left Christmas stripped and shorn of its old customs, consequently of the songs in which these were perpetuated.

As the stream of religion by the Reformation was turned into half-a-dozen channels, so Christmas lyrics came to be a personal matter in which each writer expressed his own attitude and experience. The earlier Calvinists were represented by Coverdale and the Wedderburns; the Roman Catholics by Southwell and Crashaw; the orthodox Churchmen by Bishop Hall, Giles Fletcher, Herbert, and Jeremy Taylor, and from the lay point of view, by Ben Jonson, Drummond of Hawthornden, Francis Quarles, and others.

It is interesting to note that the story of the shepherds, doubtless because of the fashion for pastorals at that time, was the aspect of the Nativity most often treated.

These compositions of Elizabethan and early Stuart days include very few real carols. Sometimes they keep so rigidly within the bounds of ecclesiastical matter that they are hymns. More often they are so elaborate in form and metaphysical in tone that they could never have been intended to be sung.

There is no doubt that Puritanism is to blame for the extinction of the practice of carol-singing, both in that it discouraged the excesses of Christmas revelry and in that it made but scant use of music as a means of religious experience. I doubt whether any good carols, either religious or secular, originated between the end of the seventeenth century and the middle of the nineteenth.

The eighteenth and early nineteenth centuries, it is true, were the great days of broadsheet publication, in which much old traditional matter was preserved, but the new carols produced during this period are scarcely worth preservation.

Within the last fifty years various attempts have been made to write carols in the medieval manner; and as deliberate imitations of old forms from which the living inspiration has nearly vanished, some of these are very good.

Printed Collections of Carols

The oldest known printed carols consist of two leaves of a collection issued by Wynkyn de Worde in 1521. The title *New Christmas Carols* suggests that earlier editions had preceded this. A unique little black song-book in the British Museum, dated 1530,[1] contains several carols; while another set of *Christmas Carols, Newly Imprinted*, issued by Richard Kele, between 1546 and 1552, now known only by extracts in Bliss's *Bibliographical Miscellanies* in 1813, is the source of several others. During the second half of the sixteenth century many other collections were made, since lost and known only by name. The Wedderburns' *Compendious Book of Godly Songs and Ballads*, in several editions, of which the first is as old as 1567, perhaps older, and several books by the musician, William Byrd, contain a few carols.

[1] Catalogued as *Bassus*, K. i.e. 1.

From the seventeenth century (1642, 1661, 1682 and undated) there are several collections of popular carols; and others were printed from time to time in *Poor Robin's Almanac*.

But the oldest carols continued to exist in manuscript until Ritson,[1] Wright,[2] and Sandys[3] did pioneer work in printing and collecting them, the process being continued by Fehr,[4] Flügel,[5] Bullen,[6] Chambers and Sidgwick,[7] and Dyboski[8]; and from a musical standpoint first by J. Stafford Smith,[9] afterwards by Nicholson and Stainer,[10] and Fuller-Maitland and Rockstro.[11] I have mentioned only the most important works, fuller bibliographies being given in the volume of Chambers and Sidgwick, and in the *Cambridge History of English Literature*, vol. ii. Information in regard to the manuscripts, published and unpublished, is to be found in Hughes Hughes' *Catalogue of Early English Music* (Sacred).

Plan of the Present Edition

In the present edition I have attempted to classify the carols according to their subject-matter; and within the various groups to arrange them, as far as may be, chrono-

[1] *Ancient Songs and Ballads*, 1790; ed. Hazlitt, 1877.
[2] Percy Society publications, vols. iv. and lxxiii.; Warton Club, vol. iv.
[3] Percy Society publications, vol. iv.; *Christmas Carols*, 1833; *Christmastide*, 1852.
[4] *Archiv für das Studium der neueren Sprachen und Literaturen*, cvi., cvii., cix.
[5] *Anglia*, xii., xxvi.; *Neuenglisches Lesebuch*, 1895.
[6] *A Christmas Garland*, 1885.
[7] *Early English Lyrics*, 1907.
[8] Early English Text Society, Extra Series, CI.
[9] *Old English Songs*, 1780.
[10] *Early Bodleian Music.*
[11] *English Carols of the Fifteenth Century*, 1891.

logically, except where it seemed advisable to show some special relationship. To the left of each carol I have put the date of its first appearance in manuscript or in print, or, failing that, the nearest approximation possible to the date of the oldest manuscript, or the time when the author flourished.

While the collection is far from complete, owing to limitations of space, I have endeavoured to include (1) all the best, and (2) all the most characteristic and representative specimens of this form of writing. The second group necessarily contains some of inferior poetic quality.

My original plan was to allow equal space to sacred carols and to secular; but the former so greatly outnumber the latter as to run into nearly half of the second part. Accordingly I have divided the sacred carols into two groups :—

I. Carols of the Nativity.

II. Carols of the Divine Mystery.

The distinction, which is perhaps not very well expressed by the titles, is between the carols which emphasize the Nativity as an historical and dramatic event, and those that dwell upon the meaning of the Incarnation. The two groups approach each other so that there might be difference of opinion as to how a few carols should be classified ; but as it was necessary to make some sort of division, and a great many carols show a strong theological element, this arrangement seemed to be the most satisfactory.

The Nativity Carols are subdivided into seven groups :—

I. Carols of the Virgin : *Virgo Rosa Virginum.*

II. Carols of the Annunciation : *Ecce Ancilla Domini.*

III. Carols of the Nativity : *In Die Nativitatis.*

IV. Carols of the Childhood of Jesus : *O Jesu Parvule.*

V. Carols of the Shepherds : *Gloria in Excelsis Deo.*

VI. Carols of the Three Kings : *Reges de Saba Venient.*

VII. Carols of the Christmas Saints : *Nunc Gaudet Ecclesia.*

I have added also in Appendix I. a few examples of Latin Christmas hymns and of Anglo-Norman and French carols; and in Appendix II., specimens of carols not related in subject-matter to Christmas.

In dealing with the individual texts, I have tried to preserve as far as possible the effect of the original; and to this end have allowed quaint, obsolete, and even ungrammatical expressions to stand, when they did not obscure the meaning, or could easily be explained in a footnote. With the metre I have tampered as little as possible, wishing to show the range of skill in different authors from barbaric roughness to exquisite melody.

In the case of French and Latin phrases I have retained the old forms, correcting obvious errors. They afford no difficulty to readers of these languages, and heighten the quaintness of the effect. A glossary, however, of these phrases is given at the end of Part III. My original plan of translating these in the footnotes was abandoned because of the numerous repetitions of familiar Church phrases.

A special difficulty arose in the case of carols that exist in several versions. As exact texts were out of the question here, both because of the exigencies of translation, and because their establishment would have required constant return from the printed editions to the manuscripts, and frequent repetitions of parallel versions, the best plan seemed to be to use the different forms of one poem to elucidate a corrupt or an obscure passage, and otherwise to choose what seemed the most interesting text and give only important variants in the footnotes. Sometimes choice was almost impossible among several versions identical in thought and differing only in a multitude of details.

Carols of the Divine Mystery are subdivided into the very large group in which the event of the Nativity is subordinated to the meaning of the Incarnation, *Mirabile Misterium*, and into a small group, *In Dulci Iubilo*, in which the spiritual joy of Christmas is sung, as over against the riotous mirth handed down as customary from the days of pagan Yule.

In Part III. I have included Carols of Yuletide Festivity, subdividing them into four groups that represent four aspects of Christmas celebrations:

I. Carols of Welcome and Christmas Cheer: *Proface.*

II. Carols of Health-drinking: *Wassail.*

III. Carols of the Boar's Head: *Caput Apri Defero.*

IV. Carols of Holly and Ivy: *Veni Coronaberis.*

Appendix I. contains Christmas poems of the sixteenth and seventeenth centuries which can scarcely be called carols; and Appendix II., a few modern carols in imitation of the medieval manner.

Literary Value of the Carols

In literary value the carols range from gems of religious inspiration to jogging tavern ditties. In some subjects they are over-bound to the Biblical material; in others they show vivid imagination and tender feeling. As a class the lullabies are the most beautiful, being as exquisite in form as in essence; and next to these, perhaps, come the carols of Mary. Out of something like two hundred anonymous carols there are very few that lack some beauty or quaintness or charm; and there are perhaps twenty or more that may be counted among those best songs that spring perfect out of the hearts of men.

The illustrations are reproduced from missals as follows:

MS. 18,850 (the Bedford Missal). 1420–30. "Puer natus est," p. 96. "Nunc gaudet Ecclesia," p. 121.

MS. 20,694. Fifteenth century. "Salve Regina," p. 159.

MS. 17,280. 1506. "Joseph being an aged man," p. 25.

MS. 25,695. Fifteenth century. "In Die Nativitatis," p. 41.

MS. Egerton, 1070. Fifteenth century. "Ecce Ancilla Domini," Frontispiece.

MS. 18,855. Sixteenth century. "The Boar is Dead," p. 260.

MS. 24,098. Sixteenth century. "Make we merry," p. 203.

The two last named are attributed to the Flemish artist, Gerhard Hoornbach.

PART I

CAROLS OF THE NATIVITY

VIRGO ROSA VIRGINUM[1]

Mater Salutaris

Thirteenth Century.

SAINT Mary, mother mild,
Mater salutaris,
Fairest flower of any field,
Vere nuncuparis,
Through Jesu Christ thou wert with child,
Thou bring me of my thoughtës wild,
Potente,
That maketh me to death [to] go
Repente.
My thought is wild as is the roe,
Luto gratulante,
She worketh me full muchel woe,
Illaque favente ;
But if He willë wend me fro
I ween my heart breaketh a-two,
Fervore ;
I tamëd[2] am both day and night,
Dolore.
Jesu, through Thy muchel might
Omnia fecisti.

[1] See note. [2] *Text:* am ifaiht.

The Holy Ghost in Mary light
Sicut voluisti,
Therefore He is yclept our Driht;[1]
Jesu, bring my thought to Christ
Constanter,
That it be stable and not changeable,
Fraudenter.
Jesu Christ, Thou art on loft,[2]
Digno Tu scandente,
Heaven and earth Thou havest ywrought,
Victore triumphante,
Mankind with Thy body a-bought,
Thou wouldst not him have lost for nought,
Nec dare;
And gave the blood that was so good,
Tam gnare.
Sweetë lady, flower of all,
Vere consolatrix,
Thou be mine help that I ne[3] fall,
Cunctis reparatrix.
Mildest queen and best ycorn,[4]
Night and day thou be me forn[5]
Precantis.
Give me grace to see thy face,
Infantis,
That I through thy sweetë bene,[6]
Tutrix orphanorum,
May leavë all this worldës teen,[7]
Solamen miserorum.
And to thee, Lady, may I take

[1] Lord. [2] On high. [3] Not.
[4] Chosen. [5] Be for me. [6] Prayer.
[7] Trouble.

And my sins [may] all forsake,
Volente,
That I ne missë of thy bliss,
Poscente.

Enixa est Puerpera

1425–50.

A LADY that was so fair and bright,
Velut maris stella,
Brought forth Jesu full of might,
Parens et puella.

Lady, flower of allë thing,
Rosa sine spina,
That barest Jesu, Heaven-King,
Gracia Divina.

All this worldë was forlore,
Eva peccatrice,
Till that Jesu was ybore,
De te, genetrice.

Of all women thou art best,
Felix fecundata,
To all weary thou art rest,
Mater honorata.

Well I wot He is thy Son,
Ventre quem portasti ;
There will He grant thee thy boon,
Infans quem lactasti.

How sweet He is, how meek He is
Nullus memoravit;
In heaven He is and heaven[ly] bliss
Nobis preparavit.

Of all women thou bearest the prize,
Mater gratiosa,
Grant us allë Paradise,
Virgo gloriosa.

As Dew in April

Fifteenth Century.

I SING of a maiden
That is makeless;[1]
King of all kings
To her Son she ches.[2]
He came all so still
Where His mother was,
As dew in April
That falleth on the grass.
He came all so still
To His mother's bower,
As dew in April
That falleth on the flower.
He came all so still
Where His mother lay,
As dew in April
That falleth on the spray.
Mother and maiden
Was never none but she;
Well may such a lady
Godës mother be.

[1] Matchless. [2] Chose.

M and A and R and I[1]

Fifteenth Century.

M and A and R and I,
Singen I will a new song.

Of these four letters purpose I,
M and A and R and I;
They betoken maid Mary,
All our joy of her sprang.

Withouten sin of her body,
—*M and A and R and I*—
Of her was born a king truly,
The Jews did to death with wrong.

Upon the mount of Calvary,
—*M and A and R and I*—
There they beat His bare body,
With scourges that were sharp and long.

Our dear Lady she stood Him by,
—*M and A and R and I*—
And wept water full bitterly;
Tears of blood followed ever among.

God that sitteth above the sky,
With M and A and R and I,
Save now all this company,
And send us joy and bliss among!

[1] See note.

Ave Maris Stella

Fifteenth Century.

Ave maris stella,
The star on the sea,
Dei mater alma
Blessed may she be!

Atque semper virgo,
Pray thy Son for me,
Felix celi porta,
That I may come to thee.

Gabriel, that archangel,
He was messenger,
So fair he greeted our Lady,
With an *ave* so clear.

Hail be thou, Mary,
Be thou, Mary,
Full of Godës grace,
And queen of mercy!

All that are to greet
Withouten deadly sin,
Forty days of pardon
God granteth him.

There is no Rose of such Virtue[1]

Fifteenth Century.

There is no rose of such virtue,
As is the rose that bare Jesu,
Alleluia!

[1] See note.

For in this rose containëd was
Heaven and earth in little space,
Res miranda!

By that rose we may well see,
There be one God in Persons Three,
Pares forma.

The angels sungen the shepherds to,
Gloria in excelsis Deo,
Gaudeamus!

Leave we all this worldly mirth,
And follow we this joyful birth,
Transeamus.

Of a rose, a lovely rose,[1] *And of a rose I sing a song*[2]

Fifteenth Century.

HEARKEN to me, both old and ying,
How a rose began to spring;
A fairer rose to my liking
Sprang there never in kingës land.

Six branches are on that rose beam,
They be both bright and sheen;
The rose is called Mary, heaven's queen,
Of her bosom a Blossom sprang.

[1] See note.

[2] Where I have used the MS. heading, sometimes as here a couplet, as a title, it is printed without capitals.

The first branch was of great might,
That sprang on Christmas night.
The star[1] shone over Bethlehem bright,
 That men might see both broad and long.

The second branch was of great honour,
That was sent from heaven's tower;
Blessed be that fair flower,
 Break it shall the fiendës bonds.

The third branch widë spread,
Where Mary lay in her bed;
The bright star three kingës led
 To Bethlehem, where that branch they found.

The fourth branch sprang into hell,
The fiendës boast for to fell,
There might no soulë therein dwell,
 Blessed be that time that branch sprang.

The fifth branch was fair in foot,
It sprang to heaven, top and root,
There to dwell and be our bote[2]
 And yet is seen in priestës hands.

The sixth branch by and by,
It is the five joys of mild Mary.
Now Christ save all this company,
 And send us good life and long!

[1] MS. streme=sterne? Help.

This Rose is Railed[1] on a Ryse[2]

About 1450.

Of a rosë singë we:
Misterium mirabile.

THIS rose is railëd on a ryse,
He hath bought the Prince of price,
And in this time sooth it is,
Viri sine semine.

This rose is red of colour bright,
Through whom our joy began alight,
Upon a Christës mass night,
Claro David germine.

Of this rose was Christ ybore,
To save mankind that was forlore,
And us all from sin its sore,
Prophetarum carmine.

This rose, of flowers she is the flower,
She will not fadë for no shower,
To sinful men she sent succour,
Mira plenitudine.

This rosë is so fair of hue,
In maid Mary that is so true,
Yborne was Lord of [all] virtue,
Salvator sine crimine.

[1] Set. [2] Branch.

Hail Mary, full of grace, mother in virginity

Fifteenth Century.

THE Holy Ghost is to thee sent
From the Father Omnipotent,
Now is God within thee went,
The angel said "Ave."

When the angel *ave* began,
Flesh and blood together ran;
Mary bare both God and man,
Through virtue and pure dignity.

So saith the gospel of Saint John:
God and man is made but one,
In flesh and blood, body and bone,
One God in Persons Three.

And the Prophet Jeremy
Told in his prophecy
That the Son of Mary
Should die for us on the Rood-tree.

He to us much joy did grant
And of peace on earth no want,
Since the birth of this Infant
In the land of Galilee.

Mary grant to us thy bliss
Where thy Son His dwelling is;
For what we have done amiss
Pray for grace for charity. Amen.

Nowell, ell, ell, ell, ell, ell, ell, ell, ell, ell, ell,
Mary was greeted by Gabriel

Fifteenth Century.

Mary mother, meek and mild,
Fro shame and sin that ye us shield,
For great on ground ye go with child,
Gabriele nuncio.

Mary mother, be not adread,
Jesu is in your body bred,
And of your breast He will be fed,
Cum pudoris lilio.

Mary mother, the fruit of thee
For us was nailëd on a tree,
In heaven is now His majesty,
Fulget Resurreccio.

Mary mother, the thirdë day
Up He rose, as I you say,
To hell He took the rightë way,
Motu fertur proprio.

Mary mother, after thy Son,
Up thou styest [1] with him to wone ; [2]
The angels were glad when thou wert come,
In celi palacio.

[1] Ascendest. [2] Dwell.

Alma Redemptoris Mater[1]

Fifteenth Century.

As I lay upon a night,
My thought was on a bird[2] so bright (Alleluia !)
That men call Mary full of might,
Redemptoris Mater.

To her came Gabriel with light,
And said, " Hail be thou, blissful wight (Alleluia !),
To be called now art thou dight[3]
Redemptoris Mater."

At that word that lady bright
Anon conceived God full of might (Alleluia !);
Then men wist well that she hight
Redemptoris Mater.

When Jesus on the Rood was pight,[4]
Mary was doleful of that sight (Alleluia !)
Till she saw Him rise upright,
Redemptoris Mater.

Jesu, that sittest in heaven light,
Grant us to come before Thy sight [Alleluia !]
With that bird that is so bright,
Redemptoris Mater.

[1] See note. [2] Lady. [3] Ready. [4] Placed.

Salve regina, mater misericordie

Fifteenth Century.

O BLESSEDFUL bird, full of grace,
To all mankind thou art solace,
Queen of heaven in every place,
Salve.

To our health thou bare a Child,
And yet with sin wert never [de]filed,
Mary mother, meek and mild,
Salve.

From the fiend thou us defend,
And of sin thou us amend;
Mary, thy mercy thou to us send,
Salve.

O worthy wight, we worship thee,
Full of mercy and of pity;
Wherefore we sing in each degree,
Salve.

And let us not from thee fall,
And thereto we cry and also call,
Both young and old, great and small,
Salve.

And bring us to thy Son's bliss,
Where that thy dwelling is,
Of that we pray thee that we not miss,
Salve.

A, a, a, a,
Nunc gaudet Maria

Fifteenth Century.

MARY is a lady bright,
She hath a Son of mickle might,
Over all this world she is light,
Bona natalicia.

Mary is so fair of face,
And her Son so full of grace,
In heaven [may] He make us a place,
Cum sua potencia.

Mary is so fair and bright,[1]
And her Son so full of might,[1]
Over all this world He is light,[1]
Bona voluntaria.

Mary is both good and kind,
Ever on us she hath mind,
That the fiend shall us not bind [2]
Cum sua malicia.

Mary is queen of every thing,
And her Son a lovely king;
God grant us all [a] good ending;
Regnat Dei gracia.

[1] *Text:* swote—boot—boot. [2] *Text:* shend=hurt.

Novus Sol de virgine
Reluxit nobis odie

About 1450.

THOU holy daughter of Sion,
Princess of Jerusalem,
To-day sprang of thee alone
The grain [1] of Jesse in Bethlehem.

This day also the bright star
That Balaam gan so to magnify
Arose of thee to stint [2] our war,
And in darkness us to gye.[3]

Thou art also above each one
A mother and a maiden true,
And the yard eke of Aaron
That bore this day a bourgeon new.

The orient light of Nazareth
Thou art also, to stint [2] our strife,
That broughtest forth against death
This day the soothfast Man of Life.

Thou art eke the fleece of Gideon
Ydewëd with the Holy Ghost,
The chaste temple of Solomon,
Clear as crystal in every coast.[4]

[1] Seed. [2] Stop. [3] Guide. [4] Side.

Thou art eke the joy of Israel,
To stint all our oldë sorrow,
The gate the which Ezekiel
Saw always closed, both eve and morrow.

And thou art eke the purple rose
That whilom grew in Jericho;
The Father's wisdom to enclose
Thou were the temple and tower also.

Singë we, singë we,
Regina celi, letare

Fifteenth Century.

Holy maiden, blessed thou be,
Godës Son is born of thee;
The Father of heaven worship we,
Regina celi, letare.

Hail, wife! Hail, maiden! Hail, bright of blee![1]
Hail, daughter! Hail, mater! Hail, full of pity!
Hail, chosen to the Persons Three!
Regina celi, letare.

Thou art empress of heaven so free,
Worthy maiden in majesty;
Now worship we the Trinity,
Regina celi, letare.

Lady so lovely, so goodly to see,
So buxom[2] in thy body to be,
Thou art His mother for humility,
Regina celi, letare.

[1] Face. [2] Obedient.

These been courteous kings of solemnity,[1]
They worshipped thy Son with humility;
Mildë Mary, thus redë [2] we,
Regina celi, letare.

So gracious, so precious in royalty,
Thus gentle, thus good, thus findë we
There is none such in no country,
Regina celi, letare.

And therefore kneel we down on our knee,
This blessed birth worship we;
This is a song of humility,
Regina celi, letare.

Sing we to this merry company,
Regina celi, letare

Before 1529.[3]

O QUEEN of heaven, thou sittest in thy see,[4]
O comfort of all captivity,
Right causeth us all to sing to thee,
Regina celi, letare.

O blessed branch of humility,
O causer of all felicity,
With joy and gladness sing we to thee,
Regina celi, letare.

[1] *Text:* solunte.
[2] Counsel.
[3] See note.
[4] Domain.

Benign lady, blessed may thou be,
That barest God in virginity;
Therefore sing we unto thee,
Regina celi, letare.

A song upon, Now must I sing, &c.[1]

Fifteenth Century.

Nowell, nowell, nowell, sing we with mirth,
Christ is come well, with us to dwell,
By His most noble birth.

UNDER a tree, in sporting me
Alone by a wood-side,
I heard a maid that sweetly said,
"I am with child this tide."
Nowell, nowell, nowell, sing we with mirth,
Christ is come well, with us to dwell,
By His most noble birth.

"Graciously conceived have I
The Son of God so sweet;
His gracious will I put me till,[2]
As mother Him to keep."
Nowell, nowell, nowell, sing we with mirth,
Christ is come well, with us to dwell,
By His most noble birth.

"Both night and day, I will Him pray,
And hear His laws ytaught,
And every deal His true gospel
In His apostles fraught."

[1] See note. [2] To.

Nowell, nowell, nowell, sing we with mirth,
Christ is come well, with us to dwell,
By His most noble birth.

" This ghostly case doth me embrace,
Without despite or mock,
With my darling, lullay to sing,
And lovely Him to rock."
Nowell, nowell, nowell, sing we with mirth,
Christ is come well, with us to dwell,
By His most noble birth.

" Without distress, in great lightness,
I am both night and day;
This heavenly Fode,[1] in His childhood,
Shall daily with me play."
Nowell, nowell, nowell, sing we with mirth,
Christ is come well, with us to dwell,
By His most noble birth.

" Soon must I sing, with rejoicing,
For the time is all run,
That I shall child, all undefiled,
The King of heaven's Son."
Nowell, nowell, nowell, sing we with mirth,
Christ is come well, with us to dwell,
By His most noble birth.

[1] Nursling, creature.

Puer nobis natus est, De virgine Maria

About 1456.

Be glad, lordings, be ye more and less,
I bring you tidings of gladness,
As Gabriel me beareth witness,
Dicam vobis quia.

I bring you tidings that be good,
Mary hath borne a blissful Fode,
That bought us all upon the Rood,
Sua morte pia.

For the trespass of Adam,
Fro the Father of heaven He came,
Hereto to myrthë us began,
Teste profecia.

Mary, mother and lief virgin,
That bare a child withouten sin,
Keep us all fro hellë pain,
De virgine Maria.

She may be called a Sovereign Lady[1]

1530.

She may be called a sovereign lady,
That is a maid and beareth a baby.

A maid peerless hath born God's Son;
Nature gave place

[1] Printed in the book known as *Bassus*, in the British Museum, K. 1, e. 1, which contains the bass part of a song-book.

When ghostly grace
Subdued reason.
She may be called a sovereign lady,
That is a maid and beareth a baby.

As for beauty or high gentry, she is the flower,
By God elect,
For this effect,
Man to succour.
She may be called a sovereign lady,
That is a maid and beareth a baby.

Of virgins queen, lodestar of light,
Whom to honour
We ought endeavour
Us day and night.
She may be called a sovereign lady,
That is a maid and beareth a baby.

Virgo, rosa virginum, Tuum precor Filium

Before 1536.

QUEEN of heaven, blessed may thou be,
For Godës Son born He was of thee,
For to make us free.
Gloria Tibi, Domine!

Jesu, God's Son, born He was
In a crib with hay and grass,
And died for us on the Cross.
Gloria Tibi, Domine!

To our Lady make we our moan,
That she may pray to her dear Son,
That we may to His bliss come.
Gloria Tibi, Domine!

"*Marvel not, Joseph, on Mary mild;*[1] *Forsake her not though she be with child*"

Temp. Henry VII. or VIII.

" I, JOSEPH, wonder how this may be,
That Mary waxed great when I and she
Ever have lived in chastity;
If she be with child, it is not by me."
" *Marvel not, Joseph.*"

" The Holy Ghost, with merciful distense,[2]
In her hath entered without offense,
God and man conceived by His presence,
And she virgin pure without violence.
Marvel not, Joseph."

" What the angel of God to me doth say,
I, Joseph, must and will humble obey,
Else privily I would have stolen away;
But now will I serve her till I die."
" *Marvel not, Joseph.*

Joseph, thou shalt her maid and mother find,
Her Son Redemptor of all mankind,
Thy forefathers of pains to unbind;
Therefore muse not this matter in thy mind.
Marvel not, Joseph."

[1] See note. [2] *Seemingly a unique form for* distension.

Joseph being an Aged Man

Joseph being an Aged Man[1]

Traditional.

JOSEPH being an aged man truly,
He married a virgin fair and free;
A purer virgin could no man see
  Than he chose for his wife and dearest dear.

The Virgin was pure, there was no nay,
The Angel Gabriel to her did say,
" Thou shalt conceive a Child this day,
  The which shall be our dearest dear."

The Angel no sooner this message said
But all in heart she was afraid :
" How may this be, and I a pure maid ?
  Say then to me, my dearest dear."

" The Holy Ghost, Mary, shall come unto thee,
The power of it shall overshadow thee,
And thou shalt bear a Son truly,
  The which shall be our dearest dear."

Joseph being a perfect mild man,
Perceiving that Mary with child was gone,
Said, " Tell to me, Mary, and do not frown,
  Who hath done this, my dearest dear ? "

Then answered Mary meek and mild :
" I know no father unto my child
But the Holy Ghost, and I undefiled;
  That hath done this, my dearest dear."

1 See note.

But Joseph thinking her most unjust,
Yielding her body to unlawful lust,
Out of his house he thought for to thrust
His own true love, his dearest dear.

But whilst in heart he thought the same,
The Angel Gabriel to him came,
As he lay sleeping on a frame,
Still dreaming on his dearest dear,

Who said, " Fear not to take to thee
Thy true and faithful wife Mary;
Most true and faithful is she to thee,
Then turn not away thy dearest dear."

When Joseph arose from his sleep so sound,
His love to Mary did more abound,
He would not for ten thousand pound
Forsake his love and dearest dear.

They livëd both in joy and bliss;
But now a strict commandment is,
In Jewry land no man should miss
To go along with his dearest dear,

Unto the place where He was born,
Unto the emperor to be sworn,
To pay a tribute that is duly known,
Both for himself and his dearest dear.

And when they were to Bethlehem come,
The inns were filled, both all and some,
For Joseph entreated them every one,
But could get no bed for his dearest dear.

Then were they constrainëd presently
Within a stable all night to lie,
Where they did oxen and asses tie
    With his true love and dearest dear.

The Virgin pure thought it no scorn
To lie in such a place forlorn;
But against the next morning our Saviour was born,
    Even Jesus Christ, our dearest dear.

The King of all power in Bethlehem born,
Who wore for our sakes a crown of thorn;
Then God preserve us both even and morn,
    For Jesus' sake, our dearest dear!

ECCE ANCILLA DOMINI[1]

Nowell, ell, ell, ell, ell, ell, ell, ell, ell, ell,
ell, ell, ell, ell, ell, ell

Fifteenth Century.

NOWELL, ell, both old and ying,[2]
Nowell, ell, now may we sing
In worship of our heaven[ly] King,
Almighty God in Trinity.

Listen, lordings, both lief and dear,
Listen, ladies, with glad cheer,
A song of mirth now may ye hear,
How Christ our brother He would be.

An angel from heaven was sent full snell,[3]
His name is clepëd Gabriel,
His errand he did full snell,
He sat on knee and said " Ave."

And he said : " Mary, full of grace,
Heaven and earth in every place,
Within the time of little space,
Reconcilëd it should be."

[1] See note. [2] Young. [3] Quickly.

Mary stood still as any stone,
And to the angel she said anon:
"Then heard I never of man [his] moan,
Methinketh wonder thou sayest to me."

The angel answered anon full well:
"Mary dread thee never a deal,
Thou shalt conceive a child full well,
The Holy Ghost shall shadow thee."

Mary on breast her hand she laid,
Still she stood and thus she said:
"Lo me here, God's own handmaid,
With heart and will and body free."

Mary mother, maiden mild,
For the love all of thy Child,
Fro Hellë pit thou us shield;
Amen, amen, now singë we.

Regina celi, letare

Fifteenth Century.

GABRIEL, that angel bright,
Brighter than the sun is light,
From heaven to earth he took his flight.
Letare.

In Nazareth, that great city,
Before a maiden he kneeled on knee,
And said, "Mary, God is with thee.
Letare."

"Hail, Mary, full of grace,
God is with thee and ever was;
He hath in thee chosen a place.
Letare."

Mary was afraid of that sight,
That came to her with so great light.
Then said the angel that was so bright,
"*Letare.*"

"Be not aghast of least nor most,
In thee is conceived the Holy Ghost,
To save the souls that were for-lost.
Letare."

Nova, nova: Ave fit ex Eva

Fifteenth Century.

Gabriel of high degree,
He came down from the Trinity,
From Nazareth to Galilee,[1]
Ut nova.

He met a maiden in a place;
He kneelëd down before her face;
He said: "Hail, Mary, full of grace!"
Ut nova.

When the maiden saw all this,
She was sore abashed, ywis,
Lest that she had done amiss.
Ut nova.

[1] Cf. the carol on p. 35 for the same geographical error.

Then said the angel: "Dread not you,
Ye shall conceive in all virtue
A child whose name shall be Jesu."
Ut nova.

Then said the maid: "How may this be,
Godës Son to be born of me?
I know not of man's carnality."
Ut nova.

Then said the angel anon right:
"The Holy Ghost is on thee alight;
There is no thing unpossible to God Almight."
Ut nova.

Then said the angel anon:
"It is not fully six month agone,
Since Saint Elizabeth conceived Saint John."
Ut nova.

Then said the maid anon quickly:
"I am Godës own truly,
Ecce ancilla Domini."
Ut nova.

Make we merry this new year,
Thanking God with hearty cheer

Before 1529.

GABRIEL, brighter than the sun,
Graciously greeted that maiden free;
Through her meekness Christ have we found,
Ecce ancilla Domini.

Ave Maria, virgin bright,
We joyeth of thy virginity;
The Holy Ghost is on thee light,
Thou hast conceived thy Son so free.

Now is that maidë great with child,
Herself alone also credibly;
Fro the fiend she shall us shield;
So sayeth books in their story.

Now we should sing and say nowell,
Quia missus est angelus Gabriel

Before 1536.

From heaven was sent an angel of light,
Unto a city that Nazareth hight,
Unto a maid, a bride so bright,
And full of bliss;
Nomen Maria virginis.

The angel went forth and naught he ceased,
Before that maiden he him soon dressed,
He said: "All hail, thou art full blessed,
And gracious,
Quia tecum est Dominus!"

When Mary this heard, astonied was she,
And thought what this greeting might be.
The angel her showed of grace plenty
And great solace,
Et dixit: "Maria, ne timeas."

The angel said: "Thou maiden mild,
Thou shalt conceive and bear a child;
Thy maidenhood shall be never defiled;
    Call Him Jesus,
    Hic [erit] Altissimi Filius."

When Mary, as bright as crystal stone,
These wordës heard, [she] answered anon,
And asked how all this might be done,
    And said: "How so?
    Quia virum non cognosco."

The angel said: "Thou maiden still,
The Holy Ghost shall thee fulfill."
The maid answered with voice so shrill,
    And said meekly:
    "*Ecce ancilla Domini.*"

Soon after this, this Child was born,
In Bethlehem, in a winter's morn.
Now make we merry Him beforn,
    And sing *nowell*,
    Quia missus est angelus Gabriel!

What, heard ye not, the King of Jerusalem
Is now born in Bethlehem?

Before 1536.

I SHALL you tell a great marvel,
How an angel, for our avail,
Came to a maid, and said: "All hail!"
What, heard ye not, the King of Jerusalem
Is now born in Bethlehem?

"All hail," he said, "and full of grace,
God is with thee now in this place,
A child thou shalt bear in little space."
What, heard ye not, the King of Jerusalem
Is now born in Bethlehem?

"A child!" she said. "How may that be?
There had never no man knowledge of me."
"The Holy Ghost," he said, "shall light in thee."
What, heard ye not, the King of Jerusalem
Is now born in Bethlehem?

"And as thou art, so shalt thou be,"
The angel said, "in virginity,
Before and after in every degree."
What, heard ye not, the King of Jerusalem
Is now born in Bethlehem?

The maid answered the angel again:
"If God will that this be sayn,[1]
The wordës be to me full fain."

Said.

What, heard ye not, the King of Jerusalem
Is now born in Bethlehem?

Now will we all, in rejoicing
That we have heard this good tiding,
To that Child *Te Deum* sing:
Te Deum laudamus.

Nowell, nowell, nowell, nowell,
This is the salutation of Gabriel

Before 1536.

Tidings true, there be come new,
Sent from the Trinity
By Gabriel from Nazareth to a city of Galilee:
"A clean maiden, a pure virgin,
By her humility
Hath born the Person Second in Divinity."
Nowell, nowell, nowell, nowell,
This is the salutation of Gabriel.

When that he presented was
Before her fair visage,
In most demure and goodly wise
He did to her homage,
And said: "Lady, from heaven so high,
That Lord's [own] heritage,
For He of thee will born now be,
I am sent on the message."
Nowell, nowell, nowell, nowell,
This is the salutation of Gabriel.

"Hail, virgin celestial,
  The meekest that ever was!
Hail, temple of the Deity!
  Hail, mirror of all grace!
Hail, virgin pure! I thee ensure,
  Within a little space
Thou shalt conceive and Him receive
  That shall bring great solace."
      Nowell, nowell, nowell, nowell,
      This is the salutation of Gabriel.

Then bespake the virgin again,
  And answered womanly:
"Whatsoever my Lord commandeth me,
  I will obey truly.
  Ecce sum humilima ancilla Domini:
  Secundum verbum Tuum fiat michi."
      Nowell, nowell, nowell, nowell,
      This is the salutation of Gabriel.

A New Carol of Our Lady[1]

546-21.

Lords and ladies all bydene,[2]
  For your goodness and honour,
  will you sing all of a queen;
  Of all women she is the flower.
      Nowell, nowell, nowell, nowell,
      This said the angel Gabriel.

[1] Richard Kele's *Christmas Carols*, in Bliss's *Bibliographical Miscellanies*, 1813.
[2] Together.

Of Jesse there sprang a wight,
  Isaiah said by prophecy,
Of whom shall come a man of might,
  From death to life He will us buy.
      Nowell, nowell, nowell, nowell,
      This said the angel Gabriel.

There came an angel bright of face,
  Flying from heaven with full great light,
And said, "Hail! Mary, full of grace,
  For thou shalt bear a man of might."
      Nowell, nowell, nowell, nowell,
      This said the angel Gabriel.

Astonied was that lady free,
  And had marvel of that greeting.
"Angel," she said, "how may that be?
  For never of man I had knowing."
      Nowell, nowell, nowell, nowell,
      This said the angel Gabriel.

"Dread thou nothing, Mary mild,
  Thou art fulfilled with great virtue;
Thou shalt conceive and bear a child
  That shall be namëd sweet Jesu."
      Nowell, nowell, nowell, nowell,
      This said the angel Gabriel.

She kneelëd down upon her knee,
  With heart, thought, and mild cheer:
"As thou hast said, so may it be,
  God's handmaid I am here."
      Nowell, nowell, nowell, nowell,
      This said the angel Gabriel.

Then began her womb to spring,
  She went with child without man,
He that is lord over all thing,
  His flesh and blood of her had then.
    Nowell, nowell, nowell, nowell,
    This said the angel Gabriel.

Of her was born our Heaven-King,
  And she a maid nevertheless;
Therefore be merry and let us sing,
  For this new lord of Christmas.
    Nowell, nowell, nowell, nowell,
    This said the angel Gabriel.

The Conception of Christ[1]

Before 1567.

LET us rejoice and sing
And praise that michty King,
Whilk sent His Son of a virgin bricht.
    La-lay-la.

And on Him tuke our vile nature,
Our deadly woundës to cure,
Mankind to hold in richt.
    La-lay-la.

Saint Luke writes in his gospel,
God sent His angel Gabriel
Unto that virgin but[2] defame,
    La-lay-la.

[1] *Ane Compendious Buik of Godlie and Spirituall Sangis.* See note.
[2] Without.

For to fulfil the prophecy,
Was spousit with Joseph free;
Marie she had to name.
La-lay-la.

Thir words to her he did rehearse,
" Hail, Marie, full of grace,
The Lord God is with thee ! "
La-lay-la.

" Thou blessed virgin mild,
Thou sall conceive ane Child,
The people redeem sall He."
La-lay-la.

" Whose power and great micht
Sall be in Godës sicht,
Whilk from the Fader of micht is sent."
La-lay-la.

" Jesus His name ye call
Whilk sall be prince over all,
His kingdom sall have nane end."
La-lay-la.

Than spake that virgin free,
" Behold, how sall this be,
Seeing I know na man ? "
La-lay-la.

Than said the angel chaste,
" By the power of the Haly Ghaist,
Whilk all thing work He can."
La-lay-la.

"Elizabeth thy cousin also,
Six moneth with child can go,
At whose birth great joy sall be."
La-lay-la.

"Call him John," says the angel bricht,
Whilk is sent by Godës micht,
The Lordës way prepare sall he."
La-lay-la.

In Die Nativitatis

IN DIE NATIVITATIS[1]

Blessed be that lady bright,
That bare a child of great might,
Withouten pain, as it was right,
Maid mother Mary.

Fifteenth Century.

God's Son is born, His mother is a maid
Both after and beforn, as the prophecy said,
With ay;
A wonder-thing it is to see,
How maiden and mother one may be;
Was there never none but she,
Maid mother Mary.

This great Lord of heaven our servant is become,
Through Gabriel's steven,[2] our kind hath taken on,
With ay;
A wonder-thing it is to see,
How lord and servant one may be;
Was there never none but He,
Born of maid Mary.

Two suns together they ought to shinë bright;
So did that fair lady when Jesu in her light,[3]
With ay;

[1] See note. [2] Voice. [3] Alighted.

A wonder-thing doth befall:
The Lord that boughtë free and thrall,
Is found in an ass's stall,
By His mother Mary.

The shepherds in their region they lookëd into heaven,
They see an angel coming down, that said with mildë steven,
With ay:
"Joy be to God Almight,
And peace in earth to man is dight,[1]
For God was born on Christmas night,
Of His mother Mary."

Three kings of great noblay,[2] when that Child was born,
To Him they took the ready way, and kneelëd Him beforn,
With ay;
These three kings came fro far,
Through leading of a star,
And offered Him gold, incense and myrrh,
And to His mother Mary.

A Little Child There is Yborn

Before 1536.

Gloria Tibi, Domine,
Qui natus es de virgine!
A little child there is yborn,
Out of Jesse's stock ycorn,[3]
To save all us that were forlorn.
Gloria Tibi, Domine,
Qui natus es de virgine!

[1] Prepared. [2] Rank.
[3] Chosen. *The original reads:* Ysprounge out of Jesses more (*stock*).

Jesus that is so full of might
Yborn He was about midnight;
The angels sang with all their might:
Gloria Tibi, Domine,
Qui natus es de virgine!

Jesus is that Childës name,
Maid and mother is His dame,
And so our sorrow is turned to game.[1]
Gloria Tibi, Domine,
Qui natus es de virgine!

Three kings there came with their presents,
Of myrrh and gold and frankincense,
As clerkës sing in their sequence.
Gloria Tibi, Domine,
Qui natus es de virgine!

Now sit we down upon our knee,
And pray that Child that is so free;
And with good heartë now sing we:
Gloria Tibi, Domine,
Qui natus es de virgine!

All this time this song is best: *Verbum caro factum est*

Before 1536.

THIS night there is a Child [y]born,
That sprang out of Jesse's thorn;
We must sing and say thereforn:
Verbum caro factum est.

[1] Joy.

Jesus is the Childës name
And Mary mild is His dame,
All our sorrow is turned to game:
Verbum caro factum est.

It fell upon [the] high midnight,
The stars [they] shone both fair and bright,
The angels sang with all their might:
Verbum caro factum est.

Now kneel we down [up]on our knee,
And pray we to the Trinity,
Our help, our succour for to be.
Verbum caro factum est.

Now be we glad, and not too sad, For verbum caro factum est

Fifteenth Century.

This may I prove withouten let:[1]
When Gabriel our lady gret.[2]
On his knee he him set
So mildly:
"Thou shalt conceive this samë day,
Salvatorem mundi."

A star shone through Godës grace,
As Godës ownë will it was;
The shepherds saw in that place
Angels two;
And them among they sang a song,
"*Gloria in excelsis Deo!*"

[1] Hindrance. [2] Greeted.

The Child was born upon Yule day,
As prophets to us could say;
His mother sang *lullay*, *lullay*,
Into the east;
Therefore mankind withouten end
Sing, "*Verbum caro factum est.*"

And then by tokening of a star,
Three kings there camë from [a]far,
And offered frankincense and myrrh
To Christ so free;
Then they said with merry cheer,
"*Mane nobiscum, Domine.*"

Therefore pray we every one
To the Bairn that time was born,
He save us all from shame and scorn,
In peace and rest;
And all mankind withouten end,
Sing, "*Verbum caro factum est.*"

Eia Jesus hodie
Natus est de virgine

Fifteenth Century.

Blessed be that maid Mary,
Born He was of her body,
Godës Son that sitteth on high,
Non ex virili semine.

In a manger of an ass
Jesu lay and lullëd was,
Hardë painës for to pass,
Pro peccante homine.

Kingës came fro divers land,
With great giftës in their hand,
In Bethlehem the Child they found,
Stelle ducti lumine.

Man and child, both old and ying,
Now in His blissful coming,
To that Child may we sing,
Gloria Tibi, Domine!

Nowell, nowell, in this hall,
Make merry, I pray you all,
Unto the Child may we call,
Ullo sine crimine.

Christo paremus canticam, excelsis gloria

About 1500.

When Christ was born of Mary free,
In Bethlehem, in that fair city,
Angels sungen with mirth and glee,
"*In excelsis gloria!*"

Herdmen beheld these angels bright,
To them appearëd with great light,
And said, "God's Son is born this night,
In excelsis gloria!"

This King is come to save [His] kind,
As in Scripturs we [may] find;
Therefore this song have we in mind,
"*In excelsis gloria!*"

Then, Lord, for Thy great grace,
[Grant us] the bliss to see Thy face,
Where we may sing to Thee solace,
In excelsis gloria!

Man, be glad in hall and bower,
This time was born our Saviour

Fifteenth Century.

In this time Christ[1] hath us sent
His own Son in present,
To dwellë with us verament,
To be our help and succour.

In this time rose a star clear,
Over Bethlehem, as bright as fire,
In token that He had no peer,
Lord God, king and emperor.

In this time it is befall,
He that diëd for us all,
Born He was in ass's stall,
Of Mary, that sweet flower.

[1] *For* God.

In this time came three kings,
They came fro far with richë things,
For to make their offerings,
  On their knees with great honour.

In this timë pray we
To Him that diëd on the Tree,
On us have mercy and pity,
  And bring us all to His tower.

Man, be merry as bird on berry,
And all thy care let away

Fifteenth Century.

THIS time is born a Child full good,
He that us bought upon the Rood;
He bound the devil that is so wode,[1]
  Till the dreadful Doomësday.

When the Child of mickle might
Would be born of Mary bright,
A token He sent to king and knight,
  A star that shone both night and day.

The star [it] shone as bright as fire,
Over all the world both far and near,
In token He was withouten peer;
  And peerless He shall lasten ay.

[1] Wild.

The eighth day He was circumcised,
For to fulfil the prophesie[s];
The prophets [all] with wordës wise
  Him present with rich array.

The Twelfth Day come kingës three,
Out of the East, with heartës free,
To worship Him they kneeled on knee,
  With gold and myrrh and frankincense.[1]

Nowell, ell, ell, ell,
Now is well that ever was woe

Fifteenth Century.

A BABE is born all of a may [2]
In the salvation of us,
To Him we singen both night and day,
    Veni, Creator Spiritus.

At Bethlehem, that blessed place,
The Child of bliss born He was;
Him to serve [O] give us grace,
    O lux beata Trinitas.

There came three kings out of the East,
To worship the King that is so free,
With gold and myrrh and frankincense,
    A solis ortus cardine.

[1] See note. [2] Maiden.

The herdës hearden an angel-cry,
A merry song then sungen they,[1]
" Why are ye so sore aghast ? "
Jam ortus solis cardine.

The angels came down with a cry,
A fair song then sungen they
In the worship of that Child,
Gloria tibi, Domine !

To bliss God bring us all and some, Christe, Redemptor omnium

Fifteenth Century.

In Bethlehem, that fair city,
Was born a Child that was so free,
Lord and prince of high degree,
Jam lucis orto sidere.

Jesu, for the love of Thee,
Children were slain great plenty
In Bethlehem, that fair city,
A solis ortus cardine.

As the sun shineth in the glass,
So Jesus of His mother born was
Him to serve God give us grace,
O lux beata Trinitas.

Now is He our Lord Jesus,
Thus hath He verily visited us ;
Now to make merry among us,
Exultet celum laudibus.

[1] The angels.

Now let us sing, both more and less
Of Christ's coming Deo gracias

Before 1536.

A VIRGIN pure, this is full sure,
  Gabriel did her greet,
And all her cure,[1] I am full sure,
  Ever did endure,
      Deo gracias!

A Babe was born, early by the morn,
  And laid between the ox and the ass.
The Child they knew that was born new,
  On Him they blew:
      Deo gracias!

An angel full soon sang from aboon:[2]
  Gloria in excelsis!
That lady alone might make no moan,
  For love of One,
      Deo gracias!

This Babe us bought when we were brought
  Into great thought and dreadful case;
Therefore we sing, both old and ying,
  Of Christ's coming:
      Deo gracias!

[1] Care. [2] Above.

Make we merry in hall and bower,
This time is born our Saviour

Before 1536.

In this timë God hath sent
His own Son to be present,
To dwell with us in verament,[1]
God that is our Saviour.

In this time that is befall,
A Child was born in an ox-stall,
And after He died for us all,
God that is our Saviour.

In this time an angel bright,
Met three shepherds upon a night,
He bade them go anon right,
To *God that is our Saviour.*

In this timë now pray we,
To Him that died for us on Tree,
On us all to have pity,
God that is our Saviour.

Conditor alme siderum,
Eterna Lux credencium

Before 1536.

There is a Child born of Mary,
In salvation of all us,
That we should worship every day,
With *veni, Creator Spiritus.*

[1] In verity.

In Bethlehem, in that holy place,
This blessed Child born He was,
Him to serve, He gave us grace
With *Trinitatis unitas.*

The shepherds heard that angel's song,
And worshipped God in Trinity,
That so nigh was them among,
Iam lucis orto sidere.

Each man began to cry and call,
To Him that sitteth on high,
To His bliss to bring them all,
Iesu, Salvator seculi.

Make we Joy in this Feast[1]

Fifteenth Century.

MAKE we joy in this feast, *in quo Christus natus est,*
A Patre Unigenitus, to a maiden is come to us;
Sing we of Him and say we, "Welcome, *veni, Redemptor gencium.*"
Agnoscat omne seculum, a bright star kings made come;
For to take with their presents, *verbum superum prodiens.*
A solis ortus cardine, so mighty a lord is none as He.
. . . And[2] to our Lord He hath grith.[3]
Marya ventre concepit, the Holy Ghost was ay her with;
Of her in Bethlehem now born He is, *Consors Paterni luminis,*
Alma beata Trinitas, that lay between an ox and ass,
By His mother maiden free, *gloria Tibi, Domine.*

[1] See note. [2] The Latin half of the line is missing. [3] Peace

A Carol of the Birth of Christ[1]

1521.

Come to Bethlehem[2] *and ye shall see*
Puer natus est hodie.

A woman, a maid, &c.
Sinful man, &c.
On the Cross, &c.

FAREWELL, Advent, and have good day;
Christmas is come, now go thy way.
Get thee hence! What dost thou here?
Thou hast no love of no beggar.
Thou makest us fast with evil cheer
With farewell, Advent.
Thou takest on thee more than doth the Lent,
The[n] dwellest so long that thou art shent.[2]
When *alleluia* is aloft,
I go gay and sit soft,
And then I am merry oft,
  As any bird on briar.
When *laus Tibi*[3] cometh to town,
Then me behoveth to kneel adown,
And ever to be in orison,
  As it were a friar.
Soon at Easter cometh *alleluia*,
With butter, cheese, and a tansy;[4]
It is nothing to my pay[5]
That he tarryeth so long away.

[1] Two leaves of *Christmas Carolles*, printed by Wynkyn de Worde.
[2] Blamed. [3] Lent. [4] See note. [5] Pleasure.

Might I bide Shere-Thursday
Laus Tibi shall go away;
And I have wept that I may,
Though he never come us among.

The First Nowell the Angel did Say[1]

Traditional.

THE first nowell the angel did say
Was to three poor shepherds in the fields as they lay,
In fields where they lay keeping their sheep,
In a cold winter's night that was so deep.
Nowell, nowell, nowell, nowell,
Born is the King of Israel.

They looked up and saw a star
Shining in the East beyond them far,
And to the earth it gave great light,
And so it continued both day and night.
Nowell, nowell, nowell, nowell,
Born is the King of Israel.

And by the light of that same star
Three Wise Men came from country far;
To seek for a King was their intent,
And to follow the star wherever it went.
Nowell, nowell, nowell, nowell,
Born is the King of Israel.

The star drew nigh to the North-West,
O'er Bethlehem it took its rest,

[1] See note.

And there it did both stop and stay
Right over the place where Jesus lay.
Nowell, nowell, nowell, nowell,
Born is the King of Israel.

Then did they know assuredly
Within that house the King did lie;
One entered in then for to see,
And found the Babe in poverty.
Nowell, nowell, nowell, nowell,
Born is the King of Israel.

Then entered in those Wise Men three
Most reverently upon their knee,
And offered there in his presence
Both gold and myrrh and frankincense.
Nowell, nowell, nowell, nowell,
Born is the King of Israel.

Between an ox-stall and an ass
This Child truly there born He was;
For want of clothing they did Him lay
All in the manger, among the hay.
Nowell, nowell, nowell, nowell,
Born is the King of Israel.

Then let us all with one accord
Sing praises to our heavenly Lord,
That hath made heaven and earth of nought,
And with His blood mankind hath bought.
Nowell, nowell, nowell, nowell,
Born is the King of Israel.

If we in our time shall do well,
We shall be free from death and hell;
For God hath preparëd for us all
A resting place in general.
Nowell, nowell, nowell, nowell,
Born is the King of Israel.

Out of the Orient, Crystal Skies [1]

About 1613.

Out of the orient, crystal skies
A blazing star did shine,
Showing the place where poorly lies
A blessed Babe divine,

Born of a maid of royal blood
Who Mary hight by name,
A sacred rose which once did bud
By grace of heavenly flame.

This shining star three kings did guide
Even from the furthest East,
To Bethlehem where it betide
This blessed Babe did rest,

Laid in a silly manger poor,
Betwixt an ox and ass,
Whom these three kings did all adore
As God's high pleasure was.

[1] MS. Additional 29,401, fol. 51b, 52. See note.

And for the joy of His great birth
  A thousand angels sing :
" Glory and peace unto the earth
  Where born is this new King ! "

The shepherds dwelling there about,
  Where they this news did know,
Came singing all even in a rout,
  " Falantidingdido, falantidingdido, falantidingdido ! "

O JESU PARVULE[1]

I Saw a Sweet and Silly Sight[2]

Fifteenth Century.

I SAW a sweet [and] silly[3] sight,
A blissful bride, a blossom bright
That mourning made and mirth among.
A maiden mother, meek and mild,
In cradle kept a knavë child
That softly slept; she sat and sang.
"*Lullay, lullow, lully, lullay, lully, lully, lully, lully, lully,*
Lullow, lully, lullay, baw, baw,
My bairn, sleep softly now."

This Endernight[4] *I Saw a Sight*

Fifteenth Century.

THIS endernight
I saw a sight,
A star as bright as day;
And ever among
A maiden sang,
Lullay, by-by, lullay.

[1] See note.
[2] MS. Additional 5666, fols. 4b, 5.
[3] Blessed.
[4] This other night, *i.e.* recently.

This lovely lady sat and sang and to her child gan say:
" My Son, my Lord, my Father dear, why liest Thou in hay?
Mine own dear Son,
How art Thou come,
Art Thou not God *veray?*
But nevertheless
I will not cease
To sing, *by-by, lullay*."

The Child then spake in His talking, and to His mother said:
" I callëd am a king, in crib though I be laid,
But angels bright
Down to me light,
Thou knowest it is no nay;
And of that sight
Thou mayest be light
To sing, *by-by, lullay*."

" Now, sweet Son, since Thou art King, why art Thou laid in stall?
Why hast Thou no rich bedding in some great kingës hall?
Methinketh by right,
Thou, King and Knight,
Should lie in rich array;
And then among,
It were no wrong
To sing, *by-by, lullay*."

" Mary, mother, I am thy child, though I be laid in stall,
Lords and dukes shall worship me and so shall kingës all.
Ye shall well see
That kingës three
Shall come the twelfth day;

For this behest
Give me thy breast
And sing, *by-by, lullay.*"

"Now tell me, sweet Son, I Thee pray, Thou art me lief and dear,
How should I keep Thee to Thy pay [1] and make Thee glad of cheer?
For all Thy will
I would fulfill,
Thou wittest full well, in fay;
Yet more than this,
I will Thee kiss
And sing, *by-by, lullay.*"

"My mother dear, when time it be, thou take me up aloft,
And set me right upon thy knee, and handle me full soft,
And in thine arm
Thou lap me warm,
And keep me night and day;
And if I weep,
And may not sleep,
Thou sing, *by-by, lullay.*"

"Now, sweet Son, since it is so, that all things are at Thy will,
I pray Thee grant me now a boon, if it be right and skill,[2]
That child or man
That will or can
Be merry upon this day,
To bliss them bring,
And I shall sing,
Lullay, by-by, lullay."

[1] Content. [2] Proper.

"My mother sheen, of heaven queen, your asking shall I
speed,
So that the mirth displease me not, in words nor yet in deed,
Sing what ye will,
So that ye fulfill,
My ten commandments ay;
Ay you for to please,
Let them not cease
To sing, *by, baby, lullay*."

This Endernight I saw a Sight

Fifteenth Century.

*"Ah, my dear Son," said Mary, "ah, my dear,
Kiss Thy mother, Jesu, with a laughing cheer."*

THIS endernight I saw a sight,
All in my sleep:
Mary, that may, she sang lullay
And sore did weep;
To keep she sought full fast about
Her Son from cold.
Joseph said, "Wife, my joy, my life,
Say what ye would."
"Nothing, my spouse, is in this house
Unto my pay;
My Son a king, that made all thing,
Lieth in hay.
*Ah, my dear Son," said Mary, "ah, my dear,
Kiss Thy mother, Jesu, with a laughing cheer."*

"My mother dear, amend your cheer
And now be still;

Thus for to lie it is soothly
My Father's will;
Derision, great passion,
Infinitely,
As it is found, many a wound
Suffer shall I;
On Calvary that is so high
There shall I be,
Man to restore, nailëd full sore
Upon a tree."
"*Ah, my dear Son,*" *said Mary,* "*ah, my dear,*
Kiss Thy mother, Jesu, with a laughing cheer."

"*Quid Petis, O Fili?*"

Temp. Henry VII. or VIII.

"*Quid petis, O Fili?*"
Mater dulcissima ba ba:
"*Quid petis, O Fili?*
Michi plausus oscula da da!"

So laughing in lap laid,
So prettily, so pertly,
So passingly well apaid,[1]
Full softly and full soberly,
Unto her sweet Son she said:
"*Quid petis, O Fili?*"
Mater dulcissima ba ba:
"*Quid petis, O Fili?*
Michi plausus oscula da da!"

[1] Pleased.

The mother full mannerly and meekly as a maid,
Looking on her little Son so laughing in lap laid,
So prettily, so pertly, so passingly well apaid,
So passingly well apaid,
Full softly and full soberly,
Unto her Son she said :
 " *Quid petis, O Fili?*"
 Mater dulcissima ba ba:
 " *Quid petis, O Fili?*
 Michi plausus oscula da da!"

I mean this by Mary, our Maker's mother of might,
Full lovely looking on our Lord, the Lantern of light,
Thus saying to our Saviour, this saw I in my sight;
This reason that [I] rede in now, I rede it full right.
 " *Quid petis, O Fili?*"
 Mater dulcissima ba ba:
 " *Quid petis, O Fili?*
 Michi plausus oscula da da!"

Musing on her manners so, my word was my main,
Save it pleased me so passingly that past was my pain;
Yet softly to her sweet Son methought I heard her sayn:
" Now gracious God, and good sweet Babe, yet once again this game.
 ' *Quid petis, O Fili?*'
 Mater dulcissima ba ba:
 ' *Quid petis, O Fili?*
 Michi plausus oscula da da!' "

A New Year, a New Year, a child was yborn,
Us for to saven that all was forlorn,
So blessed be the time

Fifteenth Century.

The Father of heaven His own Son He sent,
His kingdom for to claimen [on earth is He lent].
So blessed be the time.

All in a clean maiden our Lord was ylight,
Us for to saven with all His might.
So blessed be the time.

All of a clean maiden our Lord was yborn,
Us for to saven that all was forlorn.
So blessed be the time.

"Lullay, lullay, little Child, mine own dear fode,[1]
How shalt Thou suffer [to] be nailëd on the Rood?"
So blessed be the time.

"Lullay, lullay, little Child, mine own dear smart,[2]
How shalt Thou suffer the sharp spear to Thy heart?
So blessed be the time.

"Lullay, lullay, little Child, I sing all for Thy sake,
Many [a] one is the sharp shower to Thy body is shape!"
So blessed be the time.

"Lullay, lullay, little Child, fair haps Thee befall,
How shalt Thou suffer to drink eisel[3] and gall?"
So blessed be the time.

[1] Nursling. [2] Cause of grief? [3] Vinegar.

" Lullay, lullay, little Child, I sing all beforn,
How shalt Thou suffer the sharp garland of thorn ? "
So blessed be the time.

" Lullay, lullay, little Child, why weepest Thou so sore,
And art Thou [then] both God and man, what wouldest Thou be more ? "
So blessed be the time.

Blessed be the arms the Child have tucked,[1]
And also the teats the Child hath [2] sucked.
So blessed be the time.

Blessed be the mother, the Child also,
With *Benedicamus Domino.*
So blessed be the time.

Lullay, mine Liking, my dear Son, mine Sweeting, Lullay, my dear Heart, mine own dear Darling

Fifteenth Century.

I SAW a fair maiden sit and sing,
She lulled a little child, a sweet lording :
Lullay, mine Liking, my dear Son, mine Sweeting,
Lullay, my dear Heart, mine own dear Darling.

That very lord is He that made all things
Of all lords He is Lord [and] King of all kings.
Lullay, mine Liking, my dear Son, mine Sweeting,
Lullay, my dear Heart, mine own dear Darling.

[1] *Text:* bar abowt. [2] *Text:* on.

There was mickle melody at that Childës birth,
All that were in heaven's bliss, they made mickle mirth.
Lullay, mine Liking, my dear Son, mine Sweeting,
Lullay, my dear Heart, mine own dear Darling.

Angels bright they sang that night and saiden to that Child,
" Blessed be Thou, and so be she that is both meek and mild."
Lullay, mine Liking, my dear Son, mine Sweeting,
Lullay, my dear Heart, mine own dear Darling.

Pray we now to that Child, and to His mother dear,
Grant them His blessing that now maken cheer.
Lullay, mine Liking, my dear Son, mine Sweeting,
Lullay, my dear Heart, mine own dear Darling.

By-by, Lullaby.[1]

1530.

By-by, lullaby, by-by, lullaby,
Rocked I my child ;
By-by, by-by, by-by, lullaby,
Rocked I my child.

In a dream late as I lay,
Methought I heard a maiden say
And speak these words [so] mild :
" My little son, with thee I play,
And come," she sang, " by, lullaby."
Thus rocked she her child.
By-by, lullaby, by-by, lullaby,
Rocked I my child.
By-by.

[1] *Bassus*, cf. p. **22**.

Then marvelled I right sore of this:
A maid to have a child ywis.
"By-by, lullaby."
Thus rocked she her child.
By-by, lullaby, by-by, lullaby,
Rocked I my child;
By-by, by-by, by-by, lullaby,
Rocked I my child.

Mother, white as lily flower,
Your lulling lesseth my languor

Fifteenth Century.

As I up rose in a morning,
My thought was on a maid[en] ying,
That sang asleep with her lulling,
Her sweet Son, our Saviour.

As she Him held [all] in her lap,
He took her lovely by the pap,
And thereof sweetly He took a nap,[2]
And sucked His fill of the liquor.

To His mother gan He say:
"For this milk me mustë die,
It is my kind therewith to play,
My sweet mother, *par amour*."[3]

The maiden freely gan to sing,
And in her song she made mourning,
How He that is our heaven[ly] King
Should shed His blood with great dolour.

[1] See note. [2] Draught. [3] For love's sake.

"Mother, thy weeping grieveth me sore,
Save I would die, thou hadst been lore;[1]
So away, mother, and weep no more;
  Thy lulling lesseth my languor."

Such mourning as the maiden made,
I cannot tell it in this hour;
Therefore be merry and glad,
  And make us merry for our Saviour.

Lullay, My Child, and Weep no More

Fifteenth Century.

"LULLAY, my child, and weep no more,
  Sleep and be now still;
The King of bliss thy Father is,
  As it was His will."

This endernight I saw a sight,
  A maid a cradle keep,
And ever she sang and said among,
  "Lullay, my child and sleep."

"I may not sleep, but I may weep,
  I am so woebegone;
Sleep I would, but I am cold,
  And clothës have I none."

Methought I heard, the Child answered,
  And to His mother He said,
"My mother dear, what do I here?
  In crib why am I laid?

[1] Lost.

"I was born and laid beforn
Beastës, both ox and ass;
My mother mild, I am thy child,
But He my father was.

"Adam's gilt this man had spilt,[1]
That sin grieveth me sore;
Man, for thee here shall I be
Thirty winter and more.

"Dole it is to see, here shall I be
Hanged upon the Rood,
By bailiffs beaten, my wounds a-sweating,[2]
And give my flesh for good.[3]

"Here shall I be hanged on a tree,
And die as it is skill;[4]
That I have bought, less will I nought;
It is my Father's will.

"A spear so sharp shall pierce my heart,
For deeds that I have done.
Father of grace, whether Thou hast
Forgotten Thy little son?

"Without pity here shall aby,[5]
And make my flesh all blue.
Adam, ywis,[6] this death it is,
For thee and many mo."

[1] Destroyed.
[2] *Text:* baleis, to-bete . . . to-wete.
[3] *Text:* to bote=for help.
[4] Necessary.
[5] Suffer.
[6] Certainly.

In the honour of Christës birth,
Sing we all with joy and mirth [1]

1521.

In this time of Christmas,
Betwixt an ox and an ass,
A maiden delivered was
  Of Christ, her dear Son dear.

The husband of Mary
[Saint] Joseph stood her by,
And said he was ready
  To serve her if need were.

When she her dear Son see,
She set Him on her knee,
And sang, " Hither to me,
  Come buss Thy mother dear."

On her lap she Him laid,
And with her pap He played,
And ever sang the maid :
  " Come buss Thy mother dear."

With lips culling [His],
His mouth oft she did kiss,
And said : " Sweetheart mine,
  I pray You, make good cheer."

To this Child let us pray,
That born was on this day,
Of Mary, the mild may,
  To grant us all good cheer.

[1] *Christmasse Carolles* (Wynkyn de Worde).

Now sing we with angelis:
Gloria in excelsis

Before 1536.

A Babe is born, to bliss us bring.
I heard a maid lullay and sing;
She said: "Dear Son, leave Thy weeping,
Thy Father is the King of bliss."
Now sing we with angelis:
Gloria in excelsis!

"Lullay," she said, and sang also,
"Mine own dear Son, why art Thou woe?
Have I not done as I should do?
Thy grievance, tell me what it is."
Now sing we with angelis:
Gloria in excelsis!

"Nay, mother, for thee weep I nought,
But for the woe that shall be wrought
To me, ere I mankind have bought.
Was never sorrow like it, ywis."
Now sing we with angelis:
Gloria in excelsis!

"Peace, dear Son, tell me not so,
Thou art my child, I have no mo;
Should I see men my own son slo[1]?
Alas, my dear Son, what meaneth this?"
Now sing we with angelis:
Gloria in excelsis!

[1] Slay.

"My hands, mother, that ye may see,
Shall be nailed unto a tree;
My feet all so fast shall be;
  Men shall weep that shall see this."
    Now sing we with angelis:
    Gloria in excelsis!

"Ah, dear Son! hard is my hap,
To see my child that sucked my pap,
His hands, His feet, that I did wrap,
  Be so nailed, that never did amiss."
    Now sing we with angelis:
    Gloria in excelsis!

"Ah, dear mother! yet shall a spear
My heart in sunder all to-tear;
No wonder, if I careful [1] were,
  And weep full sore to think on this."
    Now sing we with angelis:
    Gloria in excelsis!

"Ah, dear Son, shall I see this?
Thou art my child, and I thy mother, ywis,
When Gabriel called me 'full of grace,'
  He told me nothing of this."
    Now sing we with angelis:
    Gloria in excelsis!

"Ah, dear mother! through mine hair
To thrust in thorns they will not spare;
Alas, mother! I am full of care,
  That ye shall see this heaviness."
    Now sing we with angelis:
    Gloria in excelsis!

[1] Sorrowful.

"Ah, dear Son, leave thy weeping!
Thou bringest my heart in great mourning;
A careful song now may I sing;
  This tidings, hard to me it is."
    Now sing we with angelis:
    Gloria in excelsis!

"Ah! peace, dear mother, I thee pray,
Comfort me all that ye may,
And sing, 'by-by, lullay, lullay,'
  To put away all heaviness."
    Now sing we with angelis:
    Gloria in excelsis!

Lullay, Jesu, lullay, lullay!
Mine own dear mother, sing lullay

Before 1536.

So blessed a sight it was to see,
How Mary rocked her Son so free;
So fair she rocked and sang "by-by."
  Mine own dear mother, sing lullay!
    Lullay, Jesu, lullay, lullay!
    Mine own dear mother, sing lullay!

"Mine own dear Son, why weepest Thou thus?
Is not Thy father King of bliss?
Have I not done that in me is?
  Your grievance, tell me what it is."
  Mine own dear mother, sing lullay!
    Lullay, Jesu, lullay, lullay!
    Mine own dear mother, sing lullay!

" Therefore, mother, weep I nought,
But for the woe that shall be wrought
To me, ere I mankind have bought.
Mine own dear mother, sing lullay!
Lullay, Jesu, lullay, lullay!
Mine own dear mother, sing lullay!

" Mother, the timë ye shall see
Th[at] sorrow shall break your heart in three,
So foul the Jews shall fare with me.
Mine own dear mother, sing lullay!
Lullay, Jesu, lullay, lullay!
Mine own dear mother, sing lullay!

" When I am naked, they will me take,
And fast bind me to a stake,
And beat me sore for man his sake.
Mine own dear mother, sing lullay!
Lullay, Jesu, lullay, lullay!
Mine own dear mother, sing lullay!

" Upon the Cross they shall me cast,
Hand and foot, nail me fast;
Yet gall shall be my drink at last;
Thus shall my life pass away.
Mine own dear mother, sing lullay!
Lullay, Jesu, lullay, lullay!
Mine own dear mother, sing lullay!

" Ah, dear mother! yet shall a spear
My heart in sunder all to-tear;
No wonder though I careful were.
Mine own dear mother, sing lullay!
Lullay, Jesu, lullay, lullay!
Mine own dear mother, sing lullay!

"Now, dear mother, sing lullay,
And put away all heaviness;
Into this world I took the way,
Again to [heaven] I shall me dress,
Where joy is without end ay,
Mine own dear mother, sing lullay!"
Lullay, Jesu, lullay, lullay!
Mine own dear mother, sing lullay!

Lullay, Lullay, Thou Little Tiny Child[1]

1534.

Lullay, lullay, Thou little tiny Child,
By-by, lullay, lullay,
By-by, lullay, lullay.

O SISTERS two
How may we do
For to preserve this day
This poor youngling,
For whom we do sing
By-by, lullay, lullay?

Herod the King,
In his raging,
Charged he hath this day
His men of might
In his own sight
All young children to slay.

1 *Pageant of the Shearmen and Tailors, Coventry Corpus Christi Plays.*

That woe is me,
Poor Child, for Thee
And ever moan, and may
For Thy parting,
Neither say nor sing
By-by, lullay, lullay.

An Old Carol, with Lullaby[1]

1575.

My sweet little Baby, what meanest Thou to cry?
Be still, my blessed Babe, though cause Thou hast to mourn,
Whose blood most innocent to shed the cruel king hath sworn;
And lo, alas! behold what slaughter he doth make,
Shedding the blood of infants all, sweet Saviour, for Thy sake.
A King, a King is born, they say, which King this king would kill.
O woe and woeful heavy day when wretches have their will!
Lulla, la-lulla, lulla, lullaby.

Three kings this King of kings to see are come from far,
To each unknown, with offerings great, by guiding of a star;
And shepherds heard the song which angels bright did sing.
Giving all glory unto God for coming of this King,
Which must be made away—King Herod would Him kill.
O woe and woeful heavy day when wretches have their will!
Lulla, la-lulla, lulla, lullaby.

[1] Byrd's *Psalmes, Songs and Sonets, etc.*

Lo, lo, my little Babe, be still, lament no more;
From fury Thou shalt step aside, help have we still in store;
We heavenly warning have some other soil to seek;
From death must fly the Lord of life, as lamb both mild and
meek;
Thus must my Babe obey the king that would Him kill.
O woe and woeful heavy day when wretches have their will!
Lulla, la-lulla, lulla, lullaby.

But Thou shalt live and reign, as sibyls hath foresaid,
As all the prophets prophesy, whose mother, yet a maid
And perfect virgin pure, with her breasts shall upbreed
Both God and man that all hath made, the Son of heavenly
seed,
Whom caitiffs none can 'tray, whom tyrants none can kill.
O joy and joyful happy day when wretches want their will!
Lulla, la-lulla, lulla, lullaby!

Shall I, mother, shall I, shall I do so?[1]
Shall I die for man his sake,
And I never sinned thereto?

Before 1536.

I was born in a stall
Between beastës two,
To this world brought in thrall,
To live in care and woe.
Shall I, mother, shall I, shall I do so?
Shall I die for man his sake,
And I never sinned thereto?

[1] See note.

When I was eight days old,
  The law fulfilled I tho,[1]
Circumcised as a child;
  Then began all my woe.
    Shall I, mother, shall I, shall I do so?
    Shall I die for man his sake,
    And I never sinned thereto?

Though my Father be a king,
  Myself I went him fro,
Into this world to suffer many a thing—
  See, man, what thou hast do![2]
    Shall I, mother, shall I, shall I do so?
    Shall I die for man his sake,
    And I never sinned thereto?

Man, I am thy friend ay;
  Thyself art thy foe;
To my Father look thou pray,
  And leave thy sins that thou hast do.
    Shall I, mother, shall I, shall I do so?
    Shall I die for man his sake,
    And I never sinned thereto?

The Jews were so fell,
  That to Judas could they go;
They kissed me, as I you tell,
  "Hail, king!" said they tho.
    Shall I, mother, shall I, shall I do so?
    Shall I die for man his sake,
    And I never sinned thereto?

[1] Then. [2] Done.

They bound me to a pillar anon,
  Hand and foot, both two;
They scourgëd me with scourges soon;
  The blood ran my body fro.
    Shall I, mother, shall I, shall I do so?
    Shall I die for man his sake,
    And I never sinned thereto?

They clothed me in a mantel red,
  From the top to the toe,
With a crown of thorn on my head;
  With staves they beat it thereto.
    Shall I, mother, shall I, shall I do so?
    Shall I die for man his sake,
    And I never sinned thereto?

They brought me into Caiaphas' hall,
  Where he was bishop tho;
False witness on me they 'gan call.
  Mother, what shall I do?
    Shall I, mother, shall I, shall I do so?
    Shall I die for man his sake,
    And I never sinned thereto?

I took the Cross on my back full still;
  To Calvary then must I go;
I set it down upon an hill,
  With other crosses mo.
    Shall I, mother, shall I, shall I do so?
    Shall I die for man his sake,
    And I never sinned thereto?

They hanged me up [in] that tide;
  Hands and feet they nailed also;
And a thief on every side,
  To liken my body to.
    Shall I, mother, shall I, shall I do so?
    Shall I die for man his sake,
    And I never sinned thereto?

With a spear both sharp and keen
  They clave my heart in two;
Water and blood thereout ran—
  See, man, what thou hast do!
    Shall I, mother, shall I, shall I do so?
    Shall I die for man his sake,
    And I never sinned thereto?

With a spear both sharp and good
  They clave my heart in three,
Then yielded I up the ghost and died,
  That here all men may see.
    Shall I, mother, shall I, shall I do so?
    Shall I die for man his sake,
    And I never sinned thereto?

God that died on the Rood,
  And spread His arms in the East,
Send us all His blessing,
  And send us all good rest!
    Shall I, mother, shall I, shall I do so?
    Shall I die for man his sake,
    And I never sinned thereto?

Ane Sang of the Birth of Christ, with the tune of Baw Lulalaw[1]

About 1567.

I COME from heaven to tell
The best nowells that ever befell;
To you thir tidings true I bring,
And I will of them say and sing.

This day to you is born ane child,
Of Mary meek and virgin mild;
That blessed bairn, benign and kind,
Sall you rejoice, baith heart and mind.

It is the Lord Christ, God and man,
He will do for you what He can;
Himself your Saviour He will be,
Fra sin and hell to make you free.

He is our richt salvation
From everlasting damnation,
That ye may sing in glory and bliss
For ever mair in heaven with His.

Ye sall Him find but[2] mark or wring,[3]
Full simple in ane crib lying;
So lies He whilk you has wrocht,
And all this warld made of noch

[1] *Ane Compendious Buik of Godlie Psalmes and Spirituall Sangis*, cf. note on p. 38.
[2] Without.
[3] Defect

Let us rejoice and be blithe,
And with the herds go full swithe,[1]
And see what God of His grace has done,
Through Christ to bring us to His throne.

My soul and life, stand up and see
Wha lies in ane crib of tree.
What babe is that so gude and fair?
It is Christ, God's Son and Heir.

Welcome now, gracious God of micht,
To sinners vile, puir and unricht;
Thou came to save us from distress;
How can we thank Thy gentleness?

O God that made all creature,
How art Thou become so puir,
That on the hay and stray[2] will lie,
Amang the asses, oxen and kye?

And were the warld ten times so wide,
Clad over with gold and stanes of pride,
Unworthy yet it were to Thee,
Under Thy feet ane stool to be.

The silk and sandal,[3] Thee to ease,
Are hay and simple swaddling claes,
Wherein Thou glories, greatest King,
As Thou in heaven were in thy ring.

Thou took like pains temporal,
To make me rich perpetual;
For all this worldës wealth and gude
Can nothing richt Thy celsitude.

[1] Quickly. [2] Straw. [3] Thin silken stuff.

O my dear heart, young Jesus sweet,
Prepare Thy cradle in my sprite,
And I sall rock Thee in my heart,
And never mair from Thee depart.

But I sall praise Thee evermore,
With sangës sweet unto Thy glory;
The knees of my heart sall I bow,
And sing that richt *Balulalow.*

Glory be to God eternally,
Whilk gave His only Son for me,
The angels' joys for to hear,
The gracious gift of this New Year.

The Holy Well[1]

Traditional.

As it fell out one May morning,
  And upon one bright holiday,
Sweet Jesus asked of His dear mother,
  If He might go to play.

" To play, to play, sweet Jesus shall go,
  And to play pray get you gone,
And let me hear of no complaint,
  At night when you come home."

Sweet Jesus went down to yonder town,
  As far as the Holy Well,
And there did see as fine children
  As any tongue can tell.

[1] See note.

He said, " God bless you every one,
  And your bodies Christ save and see;
Little children, shall I play with you,
  And you shall play with me ? "

But they made answer to him, " No ! "
  They were lords' and ladies' sons;
And He, the meanest of them all,
  Was but a maiden's child, born in an ox's stall.

Sweet Jesus turned him around,
  And He neither laughed nor smiled,
But the tears came trickling from His eyes,
  Like water from the skies.

Sweet Jesus turned Him about,
  To his mother's dear home went He,
And said, " I have been in yonder town,
  As far as you can see.

" I have been down in yonder town,
  As far as the Holy Well,
There did I meet as fine children
  As any tongue can tell.

" I bid God bless them every one,
  And their bodies Christ save and see;
Little children, shall I play with you,
  And you shall play with me ?

" But they made answer to me, ' No ! '
  They were lords' and ladies' sons,
And I, the meanest of them all,
  Was but a maiden's child, born in an ox's stall."

" Though you are but a maiden's child,
  Born in an ox's stall,
Thou art the Christ, the King of heaven,
  And the Saviour of them all.

" Sweet Jesus, go down to yonder town,
  As far as the Holy Well,
And take away those sinful souls
  And dip them deep in hell."

" Nay, nay," sweet Jesus said,
  " Nay, nay, that may not be,
For there are too many sinful souls
  Crying out for the help of me."

(O then spoke the Angel Gabriel,
  Upon one good Saint Stephen,
" Although you're but a maiden's child,
  You are the King of heaven.") [1]

The Bitter Withy [2]

Traditional.

" As it fell out on a holy day,
  The drops of rain did fall, did fall,
Our Saviour asked leave of His mother, Mary,
  If He might go play at ball.

" To play at ball, my own dear Son,
  It's time you was going or gone,
But be sure let me hear no complaint of you,
  At night when you do come home."

[1] This stanza is sometimes omitted. [2] See note.

It was upling scorn and downling scorn!
  Oh, there He met three jolly jerdins:[1]
Oh, there He asked the three jolly jerdins
  If they would go play at ball.

"Oh, we are lords' and ladies' sons,
  Born in bower or in hall."
"Then at the very last I'll make it appear
  That I am above you all."

Our Saviour built a bridge with the beams of the sun,
  And over He gone, He gone He;
And after followed the three jolly jerdins,
  And drownded they were all three.

It was upling scorn and downling scorn!
  The mothers of them did whoop and call,
Crying out: "Mary mild, call home your child,
  For ours are drownded all!"

Mary mild, Mary mild called home her Child,
  And laid our Saviour across her knee,
And with a whole handful of bitter withy
  She gave Him slashes three.

Then He says to His mother: "Oh, the withy! oh, the withy!
  The bitter withy that causes me to smart, to smart,
Oh, the withy, it shall be the very first tree
  That perishes at the heart!"

[1] Virgins? See note.

The Cherry-Tree Carol[1]

Traditional.

I

Joseph was an old man,
  And an old man was he,
When he wedded Mary
  In the land of Galilee.

Joseph and Mary walked
  Through an orchard good,
Where was cherries and berries
  So red as any blood.

Joseph and Mary walked
  Through an orchard green,
Where was berries and cherries
  As thick as might be seen.

O then bespoke Mary,
  So meek and so mild,
" Pluck me one cherry, Joseph,
  For I am with child."

O then bespoke Joseph,
  With words most unkind,
" Let him pluck thee a cherry
  That brought thee with child."

O then bespoke the Babe
  Within His mother's womb—
" Bow down then the tallest tree
  For my mother to have some."

[1] See note.

Then bowed down the highest tree,
  Unto His mother's hand.
Then she cried, " See, Joseph,
  I have cherries at command."

O then bespake Joseph—
  " I have done Mary wrong;
But cheer up, my dearest,
  And be not cast down.

" O eat your cherries, Mary,
  O eat your cherries now,
O eat your cherries, Mary,
  That grow upon the bough."

Then Mary plucked a cherry,
  As red as the blood;
Then Mary went home
  With her heavy load.

II

As Joseph was a-walking
  He heard an angel sing:
" This night shall be born
  Our heavenly King;

" He neither shall be born
  In housen or in hall,
Nor in the place of Paradise,
  But in an ox's stall.

"He neither shall be clothed
  In purple or in pall,
But all in fair linen
  As were babies [1] all.

"He neither shall be rocked
  In silver nor in gold,
But in a wooden cradle
  That rocks on the mould.

"He neither shall be christened
  In white wine nor red,
But with fair spring water
  With which we were christenëd."

III

Then Mary took her young Son,
  And set Him on her knee:
"I pray Thee now, dear Child,
  Tell how this world shall be."

"O I shall be as dead, mother,
  As the stones in the wall;
O the stones in the streets, mother,
  Shall mourn for me all.

"Upon Easter-day, mother,
  My uprising shall be;
O the sun and the moon, mother,
  Shall both rise with me."

[1] *Or* men.

The Carnal[1] *and the Crane*

Traditional.

As I passed by a river-side,
  And there as I did rein,[2]
In argument I chanced to hear
  A carnal and a crane.

The carnal said unto the crane,
  " If all the world should turn,
Before we had the Father,
  But now we have the Son.

" From whence does the Son come ?
  From where and from what place ? "
He said : " In a manger,
  Between an ox and ass."

" I pray thee," said the carnal,
  " Tell me before thou go,
Was not the mother of Jesus
  Conceived by the Holy Ghost ? "

" She was the purest virgin,
  And the cleanest from sin ;
She was the handmaid of our Lord,
  And mother of our King."

" Where is the golden cradle
  That Christ was rocked in ?
Where are the silken sheets
  That Jesus was wrapt in ? "

1 Crow. See note. 2 Run.

"A manger was the cradle
That Christ was rocked in,
The provender the asses left,
So sweetly he slept on.

"There was a star in the west land,
So bright it did appear,
Into King Herod's chamber,
And where King Herod were.

"The Wise Men soon espied it,
And told the King on high,
A princely babe was born that night
No king could e'er destroy.

"'If this be true,' King Herod said,
'As thou tellest unto me,
This roasted cock that lies in the dish
Shall crow full fences [1] three.' [2]

"The cock soon freshly feathered was,
By the work of God's own hand,
And then three fences crowed he,
In the dish where he did stand.

"'Rise up, rise up, you merry men all,
See that you ready be,
All children under two years old
Now slain they all shall be.'

"Then Jesus, ah! and Joseph,
And Mary that was so pure,
They travelled into Egypt,
As you shall find it sure.

[1] Rounds.

[2] Cf. *Saint Stephen was a Clerk*, p. 123.

" And when they came to Egypt's land,
Amongst those fierce wild beasts,
Mary, she being weary,
Must needs sit down to rest.

" 'Come sit thee down,' says Jesus,
'Come sit thee down by me,
And thou shalt see how these wild beasts
Do come and worship me.'

" First came the lovely lion,
Which Jesu's grace did spring,
And of the wild beasts in the field,
The lion shall be the king.

" We'll choose our virtuous princes,
Of birth and high degree,
In every sundry nation,
Where'er we come and see.

" Then Jesus, ah! and Joseph,
And Mary that was unknown,
They travelled by a husbandman,
Just while his seed was sown.

" 'God speed thee, man!' said Jesus,
'Go fetch thy ox and wain,
And carry home thy corn again,
Which thou this day hast sown.'

" The husbandman fell on his knees,
Even before His face;
'Long time hast Thou been looked for,
But now Thou art come at last.

" 'And I myself do now believe,
Thy name is Jesus called;
Redeemer of mankind Thou art,
Though undeserving all.'

" 'The truth, man, thou hast spoken,
Of it thou mayst be sure,
For I must lose my precious blood
For thee and thousands more.

" 'If any should come this way,
And enquire for me alone,
Tell them that Jesus passed by,
As thou thy seed did sow.'

" After that there came King Herod,
With his train so furiously,
Enquiring of the husbandman,
Whether Jesus passed by.

" Why, the truth it must be spoke,
And the truth it must be known,
For Jesus passed by this way,
When my seed was sown.

" But now I have it reapen,
And some laid on my wain,
Ready to fetch and carry
Into my barn again."

" 'Turn back,' says the Captain,
'Your labour and mine's in vain,
It's full three-quarters of a year
Since he his seed has sown.'

"So Herod was deceived
By the work of God's own hand,
And further He proceeded
Into the Holy Land.

"There's thousands of children young,
Which for His sake did die;
Do not forbid those little ones,
And do not them deny.

"The truth now I have spoken,
And the truth now I have shown;
Even the blessed Virgin,
She's now brought forth a Son."

GLORIA IN EXCELSIS DEO[1]

Hail, Comely and Clean[2]

I. Pastor. HAIL, comely and clean! hail, young Child!
Hail, Maker, as I mean, of a maiden so mild,
Thou has worried, I ween, the warlock[3] so wild;
The false guiler of teen, now goes he beguiled.
    Lo, He merries;
Lo, He laughs, my sweeting,
A well fair meeting!
I have holden my heting.[4]
    Have a bob of cherries!

II. Pastor. Hail, suffering Saviour, for Thou has us sought!
Hail, freely fode and flower that all thing hath wrought!
Hail, full of favour, that made all of nought!
Hail! I kneel and I cower. A bird have I brought
    To my bairn.
Hail, little tiny mop![5]
Of our creed Thou art crop;[6]
I would drink on Thy cop,[7]
    Little day-starn![8]

[1] See note.
[2] *Secunda Pastorum, Towneley Plays.*
[3] Wizard, *here applied to the devil.*
[4] Promise.
[5] Child.
[6] Head.
[7] Cup.
[8] Star.

Puer natus est

III. Pastor. Hail, darling dear, full of godhead!
I pray Thee be near, when that I have need.
Hail! sweet is Thy cheer! My heart would bleed
To see Thee sit here in so poor weed,
With no pennies.
Hail! put forth Thy dall![1]
I bring Thee but a ball,
Have and play Thee withal,
And go to the tennis.

Maria. The Father of heaven, God Omnipotent,
That set all on seven,[2] His Son has He sent.
My name could He neven,[3] and light[4] ere He went.
I conceived Him full even, through might as He meant;
And now He is born.
He keep you from woe!
I shall pray Him so.
Tell forth as ye go,
And mind on this morn.

Tyrle, tyrlow, tyrle, tyrlow,
So merrily the shepherds began to blow[5]

Before 1536.

About the field they pipëd right,
So merrily the shepherds began to blow;
Adown from heaven that is so high—
Tyrle, tyrlow, [*tyrle, tyrlow*]*!*

[1] Hand.
[2] Created all things in seven days.
[3] Name.
[4] Alighted.
[5] Cf. following carol.

Of angels there came a company,
With merry songs and melody.
The shepherds anon gan them aspy.[1]
Tyrle, tyrlow, [tyrle, tyrlow]!

Gloria in excelsis, the angels sang,
And said that peace was present among,
To every man that to the faith would fong.[2]
Tyrle, tyrlow, tyrle, tyrlow!

The shepherds hied them to Bethlehem,
To see that blessed sun His beam;
And there they found that glorious stream.[3]
Tyrle, tyrlow, tyrle, tyrlow!

Now pray we to that mekë Child,
And to His mother that is so mild,
The which was never defiled,
Tyrle, tyrlow, [tyrle, tyrlow]!

That we may come unto His bliss,
Where joy shall never miss,
Then may we sing in Paradise:
Tyrle, tyrlow, [tyrle, tyrlow]!

I pray you all that be here,
For to sing and make good cheer,
In the worship of God this year.
Tyrle, tyrlow, [tyrle, tyrlow]!

[1] Began to see them. [2] Accept.
[3] star, *or* leme=light.

As I Out Rode This Enders Night[1]

1534.

As I out rode this enders night,
Of three jolly shepherds I saw a sight,
And all about their fold a star shone bright;
They sang terly terlow;
So merrily the shepherds their pipes gan blow.

Down from heaven, from heaven so high,
Of angels there came a great company,
With mirth and joy and great solemnity,
They sang terly terlow;
So merrily the shepherds their pipes gan blow.

The Jolly Shepherd Wat[2]

Before 1536.

Can I not sing but hoy,
When the jolly shepherd made so much joy.

THE shepherd upon a hill he sat,
He had on him his tabard[3] and his hat,
His tar-box, his pipe and his flagat;[4]
His name was called jolly, jolly Wat;
For he was a good herd's boy,
Ut hoy!
For in his pipe he made so much joy.
Can I not sing but hoy,
When the jolly shepherd made so much joy.

[1] *Pageant of the Shearmen and Tailors, Coventry Corpus Christi Plays.* See note. [2] See note. [3] Short coat. [4] Bottle.

The shepherd upon a hill was laid,
His dog to his girdle was tied;
He had not slept but a little braid,[1]
But "*Gloria in excelsis*" was to him said.
Ut hoy!
For in his pipe he made so much joy.
Can I not sing but hoy,
When the jolly shepherd made so much joy.

The shepherd on a hill he stood,
Round about him his sheep they yode;[2]
He put his hand under his hood,
He saw a star as red as blood.
Ut hoy!
For in his pipe he made so much joy.
Can I not sing but hoy,
When the jolly shepherd made so much joy.

"Now farewell Mall and also Will,
For my love, go ye all still
Unto[3] I come again you till,[3]
And evermore, Will, ring well thy bell."
Ut hoy!
For in his pipe he made so much joy.
Can I not sing but hoy,
When the jolly shepherd made so much joy.

"Now must I go where Christ was born;
Farewell! I come again to-morn.
Dog, keep well my sheep from the corn,
And warn well Warrock when I blow my horn."

[1] Time. [2] Went. [3] Until . . . to.

Ut hoy!
For in his pipe he made so much joy.
Can I not sing but hoy,
When the jolly shepherd made so much joy.

When Wat to Bethlehem comë was,
He sweat; he had gone faster than a pace;
He found Jesus in a simple place,
Between an ox and an ass.
Ut hoy!
For in his pipe he made so much joy.
Can I not sing but hoy,
When the jolly shepherd made so much joy.

The shepherd said anon right:
"I will go see yon ferly[1] sight,
Whereas the angel singeth on height,
And the star that shineth so bright."
Ut hoy!
For in his pipe he made so much joy.
Can I not sing but hoy,
When the jolly shepherd made so much joy.

"Jesu! I offer to Thee here my pipe,
My scrip, my tar-box, and my skirt;
Home to my fellows now will I skip,
And also look unto my sheep."
Ut hoy!
For in his pipe he made so much joy.
Can I not sing but hoy,
When the jolly shepherd made so much joy.

[1] Strange.

"Now farewell, my own herdsman Wat!"
"Yea, for God, Lady, even so I hight;[1]
Lull well Jesu in thy lap,
And farewell, Joseph, with thy round cape!"
Ut hoy!
For in his pipe he made so much joy.
Can I not sing but hoy,
When the jolly shepherd made so much joy.

"Now may I well both hope and sing,
For I have been at Christ's bearing;
Home to my fellows now will I fling;
Christ of heaven to His bliss us bring!"
Ut hoy!
For in his pipe he made so much joy.
Can I not sing but hoy,
When the jolly shepherd made so much joy.

Man, move thy mind, and joy this feast, Veritas de terra orta est

Before 1536.

As I came by the way,
I saw a sight seemly to see,
The shepherds ranging in array,
Upon the fold keeping their fee.[2]
A star they said they did espy
Casting the beams out of the East,
And angels making melody:
"*Veritas de terra orta est.*"

[1] Am called. [2] Beasts.

Upon that sight they were aghast,
  Saying these words as I say thee:
" To Bethlehem shortly let us haste
  And there we shall the truth see."
The angel said unto them all three
  To their comfort, ere ever he ceased:
" *Consolamini*, and merry be;
  Veritas de terra orta est."

From heaven, out of the highest see,
  Righteousness hath taken the way,
With mercy meddled [1] plenteously,
  And so conceived in a may;
Miranda res, this is, in fay,[2]
  So sayeth the prophet in his gest.[3]
Now is He born, Scripture doth say;
  Veritas de terra orta est.

Then passed the shepherds from that place
  And followed by the star's beam,
That was so bright afore their face,
  It brought them straight unto Bethlehem;
So bright it shone over all the realm
  Till they came there they would not rest,
To Jewry and Jerusalem;
  Veritas de terra orta est.

[1] Mingled. [2] Faith. [3] Story.

In Bethlehem, that Noble Place[1]

1546–52.

In Bethlehem, that noble place,
As by prophecy said it was,
Of the Virgin Mary full of grace,
Salvator mundi natus est.
Be we merry in this feast,
In quo Salvator natus est.

On Christmas night, an angel it told
To the shepherds keeping their fold,
That into Bethlehem with beastës would,
Salvator mundi natus est.
Be we merry in this feast,
In quo Salvator natus est.

The shepherds were [en]compassed right,
About them was a great light;
"Dread ye naught," said the angel bright,
Salvator mundi natus est."
Be we merry in this feast,
In quo Salvator natus est.

"Behold, to you we bring great joy.
For why? Jesus is born this day;
To us, of Mary, that mild may,
Salvator mundi natus est."
Be we merry in this feast,
In quo Salvator natus est.

[1] Richard Kele's *Christmas Carols.*

And thus in faith find it ye shall,
Lying poorly in an ox-stall.
The shepherds then lauded God all,
Quia Salvator mundi natus est.
Be we merry in this feast,
In quo Salvator natus est.

God Rest You Merry, Gentlemen

Traditional.

God rest you merry, gentlemen,
Let nothing you dismay,
For Jesus Christ our Saviour
Was born upon this day,
To save us all from Satan's power
When we were gone astray.
O tidings of comfort and joy,
For Jesus Christ our Saviour was born on Christmas Day.

In Bethlehem in Jewry
This blessed babe was born,
And laid within a manger
Upon this blessed morn;
The which His mother Mary
Nothing did take in scorn.
O tidings of comfort and joy,
For Jesus Christ our Saviour was born on Christmas Day.

From God our heavenly Father
A blessed angel came,

And unto certain shepherds
  Brought tidings of the same,
How that in Bethlehem was born
  The Son of God by name.
    O tidings of comfort and joy,
    For Jesus Christ our Saviour was born on
      Christmas Day.

"Fear not," then said the angel,
  "Let nothing you affright,
This day is born a Saviour
  Of virtue, power, and might;
So frequently to vanquish all
  The friends of Satan quite."
    O tidings of comfort and joy,
    For Jesus Christ our Saviour was born on
      Chritsmas Day.

The shepherds at those tidings
  Rejoicëd much in mind,
And left their flocks a-feeding
  In tempest, storm, and wind,
And went to Bethlehem straightway,
  This blessed Babe to find.
    O tidings of comfort and joy,
    For Jesus Christ our Saviour was born on
      Christmas Day.

But when to Bethlehem they came,
  Whereas this Infant lay,

They found Him in a manger
  Where oxen feed on hay;
His mother Mary kneeling
  Unto the Lord did pray.
    O tidings of comfort and joy,
    For Jesus Christ our Saviour was born on
      Christmas Day.

Now to the Lord sing praises,
  All you within this place,
And with true love and brotherhood
  Each other now embrace;
This holy tide of Christmas
  All others doth deface.
    O tidings of comfort and joy.
    For Jesus Christ our Saviour was born on
      Christmas Day.

The Shepherd's Song

A CAROL OR HYMN FOR CHRISTMAS

1600. Edmund Bolton.[1]

Sweet music, sweeter far
  Than any song is sweet,
Sweet music, heavenly rare,
  Mine ears, O peers, doth greet.
You gentle flocks, whose fleeces, pearled with dew,
  Resemble heaven, whom golden drops make bright,

[1] *England's Helicon.*

Listen, O listen, now, O not to you
 Our pipes make sport to shorten weary night;
  But voices most divine
   Make blissful harmony,
  Voices that seem to shine,—
   For what else clears the sky?
Tunes can we hear, but not the singers see,
The tunes divine, and so the singers be.

  Lo, how the firmament
   Within an azure fold
  The flock of stars hath pent,
   That we might these behold.
Yet from their beams proceedeth not this light,
 Nor can their crystals such reflection give.
What there doth make the element so bright?
 The heavens are come down upon earth to live.
  But hearken to the song.
   "Glory to glory's King,
  And peace all men among,"
   These choristers do sing.
Angels they are, as also (shepherds) be
 Whom in our fear we do admire to see.

  "Let not amazement blind
   Your souls," said he, "annoy;
  To you and all mankind
   My message bringeth joy,
For lo, the world's great Shepherd now is born,
 A blessed babe, an infant full of power;
After long night uprisen is the morn,
 Renowning Bethlehem in the Saviour."

Sprung is the perfect day,
By prophets seen afar ;
Sprung is the mirthful May,
Which winter cannot mar.
In David's city doth this Sun appear
Clouded in flesh, yet, shepherds, sit we here?

I Heard a Mess of Merry Shepherds[1]

About 1611.

I HEARD a mess of merry shepherds sing
A joyful song full of sweet delight ;
Their ditty was how that a King
In Bethlehem was born that night,
Whose mother was a virgin (fair and) bright,
And Mary hight her blessed name,
A queen of fame
Who for the fault of Adam's sin
Was brought abed even in an inn.
A joyful news let us rejoice,
With heart and voice ;
Yet how can we but weep alas,
To see between an ox and ass,
In manger poor the Babe He lies
That made the world and rules the skies.

[1] MS. Egerton, 2009-12, fol. 8.

REGES DE SABA VENIENT[1]

Now is Christmas Ycome

Fifteenth Century.

Now is Christmas ycome,
Father and Son together in one,
Holy Ghost, as ye be one,
                    in fere-a,[2]
God send us a good New Year-a!

I would you sing for an I might,
Of a Child is fair in sight,
His mother him bare this endernight
                    so still-a,
And as it was His will-a.

There came three kings fro Galilee
Into Bethlehem, that fair city,
To seek Him that ever should be
                    by right-a,
Lord and king and knight-a.

As they came forth with their offering,
They met with Herod, that moody king,
                    this tide-a,
And this to them he said-a:

[1] See note. [2] Together.

"Of whence be ye, you kingës three?"
"Of the East, as you may see,
To seek Him that ever should be
by right-a,
Lord and king and knight-a."

"When you at this child have be,
Come home again by me,
Tell me the sight that you have see,
I pray you;
Go you no other way-a."

They took their leave, both old and ying,
Of Herod, that moody king;
They went forth with their offering
by light-a,
By the star that shone so bright-a.

Till they came into the place
Where Jesus and His mother was,
Offered they up with great solace
in fere-a
Gold, incense, and myrrh-a.

The Father of heaven an angel down sent
To thiccy [1] three kings that made present
this tide-a,
And this to them he said-a.

"My Lord hath warned you every one,
By Herod king you go not home;
For an you do, he will you slone [2]
and strye-a, [3]
And hurt you wonderly-a."

[1] *Dialect still for* these. [2] Slay. [3] Destroy.

Forth then went these kingës three,
Till they came home to their country;
Glad and blithe they were all three
Of the sight that they had see
bydene-a;[1]
The company was clean-a.

Kneel we now here a-down,
Pray we in good devotion
To the King of great renown,
of grace-a,
In heaven to have a place-a.

Reges de Saba venient,
Aurum, tus, myrram offerent.
Alleluia

Fifteenth Century.

Now is the Twelfth Day ycome,
The Father and Son together are nome,[2]
The Holy Ghost, as they were wone,[3]
In fere.
God send us good New Year!

I will you sing with all my might,
Of a Child so fair in sight,
A maiden him bore this endernight,
So still;
As it was his will.

[1] Together. [2] Taken. [3] Wont.

Three kingës out of Galilee
Camen to Bethlehem, that city,
For to taken into that see [1]
By night;
It was a full fair sight.

As they came forth with their offering,
They met with Herod, that moody king;
He askëd them of their coming,
That tide,
And thus to them he said:

"Fro whence come ye, kingës three?"
"Out of the East, as thou mayst see,
To seek Him that ever shall be,
Through right,
Lord and king of might."

"When ye have at that king a-be,
Come again this way by me,
And tell me the sights that [ye] have see;
I pray,
Ye go none other way."

Of Herod, [of] that moody king,
They took their leave, of old and ying;
And forth they went with their offering
In sight,
And there they came by night.

[1] Domain.

When they came into the place
Where Jesu with His mother was,
They made offering with great solace,
Not fear,
With gold, incense and myrrh.

As they were homeward ywent,
The Father of heaven an angel sent
To those three kings that made present,
Ere day,
And thus to them gan say:

"My Lord hath warned you of your foe,
By King Herod that ye not go;
For if ye do, he will you slo,[1]
And 'tray;[2]
Ye go another way."

When they came home to their country,
Blithe and glad they were all three
Of the sights that they had see,
By night,
Jesu and Mary bright.

With treason to us[3] gan he sayn,[4]
He trowed Jesu to have slain;
Into Egypt they went full plain,
By side,
Joseph was their guide.

[1] Slay. [2] Betray.
[3] See note. [4] Say.

Into Bethlehem[1] they gan pass,
The star gan shinen in their face,
Brighter than ever shone sun in glass,
In land;
Jesu with Mary they found.

King Herod he made his vow,
Great plenty of children he slow,[2]
He meant they should a-been Jesu;
I say,
He failëd of his prey.

Herod was wode[3] in royalty;
He slew children right great plenty
In Bethlehem, that fair city,
With strife;
Nor left he none in life.

The children of Israel cried, "Wa, wa!"
The mothers of Bethlehem cried, "Ba, ba!"
Herod, that wretch, [he] laughed "A-ha!"
And said,
"The King of Jews is dead!"

Almighty God in majesty,
In one God Persons Three,
Bring us to Thy bliss that is so free,
In fere;
And send us a good New Year!
Reges de Saba venient,
Aurum, tus, myrram, offerent.

[1] See note. [2] Slew. [3] Mad.

Be merry all that be present,
Omnes de Saba venient

Before 1536.

OUT of the East a star shone bright,
For to show three kingës light,
Which had far travelled day and night
To seek that Lord that all hath sent.

Thereof heard King Herod anon,
That three kings should come through his region,
To seek a child that peer had none,
And after them soon he sent.

King Herod cried to them quickly:
" Ye go to seek a child truly;
Go forth and come again me by,
And tell me where that he is lent."[1]

Forth they went by the starry gleam,
Till they came to merry Bethlehem;
There they found that sweet Bairn—Him,[2]
That sithe for us His blood hath spent.

Balthasar kneelëd first adown
And said: " Hail, King, most of renown,
And of all kings thou bearest the crown;
Therefore with gold I Thee present."

Melchior kneeled down where he stood [3]
And said: " Hail, Lord, in Thy priesthood,
Receive incense to Thy manhood,
I bringë it with good intent."

[1] Arrived, *lit.*, landed. [2] *Text:* barn-teme=child.
[3] *Text:* in that stede=place.

Jasper kneeled down where he stood
And said: "Hail, Lord, in Thy knighthood,
I offer thee myrrh to Thy godhead,
For thou art He that all hath sent."

Now lords and ladies in rich array,
Lift up your hearts upon this day,
And ever to God let us pray,
That on the Rood was rent.

Alleluia! alleluia!
Deo Patri sit gloria

Before 1536.

THERE is a Blossom sprung of a thorn,
To save mankind that was forlorn,
As the prophets said beforn,
Deo Patri sit gloria!

There sprang a well at Mary's foot,
That turnëd all this world to boot;[1]
Of her took Jesus flesh and blood,
Deo Patri sit gloria!

From that well there stretched a stream,
Out of Egypt into Bethlehem;
God through His highness turned it again,
Deo Patri sit gloria!

There were three kings of divers lands,
They thought a thought that was strong,
Him to seek and thank among.
Deo Patri sit gloria!

[1] Help.

They came richly with their presents,
With gold, myrrh and frankincense,
As clerkës read in their sequence,
Deo Patri sit gloria!

The eldest king of them three,
He went foremost for he would see
What doomsman [1] that this should be,
Deo Patri sit gloria!

The middlemost king up he rose,
He saw a Babe in armës close;
In middle age he thought He was.[2]
Deo Patri sit gloria!

The youngest king up he stood,
He made his offering rich and good,
To Jesus Christ that shed His blood.
Deo Patri sit gloria!

There shone a star out of heaven bright,
That men of earth should deem aright
That this was Jesu full of might.
Deo Patri sit gloria!

Out of the Blossom Sprang a Thorn

Fifteenth Century.

Out of the blossom sprang a thorn,
When God himself would be born;
He let us never be forlorn,
That born was of Marie.

[1] Judge. [2] He had expected to find Him.

There sprang a well all at her foot,
That all this world is turned to good,
When Jesu Christ took flesh and blood
Of His mother Marie.

Out of the well [there] sprang a stream
From patriarch to Jerusalem,[1]
Till Christ Himself it took again [2]
Of his mother Marie.

In winter when the frost Him froze,
A poor bedding our Lord Him chose;
Between an ox and an ass
Godës Son born He was
Of his mother Marie.

It was upon the Twelfth Day,
There come three kings in rich array,
To seekë Christ where He lay
And his mother Marie.

Three kings out of divers lands,
Swithe [3] comen with hearts [full] strong,
The Child to seek [they] underfong,[4]
That born was of Marie.

The star led them a rightë way
To the Child where He lay;
He helpeth us both night and day,
That born was of Marie.

1 See note. 2 *Text:* again it nem.
3 Quickly. 4 Undertook.

Balthazar was the first king,
He broughtë gold to his offering,
For to present that richë King,
And His mother Marie.

Melchior was the second king,
He brought incense to his offering,
For to present that richë King,
And His mother Marie.

Jasper was the third king,
He brought myrrh to his offering,
For to present that rich King,
And His mother Marie.

There they offered their presents,
With gold and myrrh and frankincense,
As[1] clerks read in their sequence
In Epiphany.

Kneel we down Him beforn,
And pray we to Him that now is born,
He[1] let us never be forlorn,
That born was of Marie.

[1] *Text:* and.

Nunc gaudet Ecclesia

NUNC GAUDET ECCLESIA[1]

Welcome Yule

Fifteenth Century.

WELCOME, Yule, thou merry man, in worship
of this holy day,
Welcome be Thou, heaven's King,
Welcome, born in one morning,
Welcome, for whom we shall sing,
Welcome Yule.

Welcome be ye, Stephen and John,
Welcome, Innocents every one,
Welcome Thomas, martyred one,
Welcome Yule.

Welcome be ye, good New Year,
Welcome Twelfth Day, both in fere,
Welcome saints [both] lief and dear,
Welcome Yule.

Welcome be ye, Candlemas,
Welcome be ye, Queen of Bliss,
Welcome both to more and less,
Welcome Yule.

[1] See note.

Welcome be ye that are here,
Welcome all and make good cheer,
Welcome all another year,
Welcome Yule.

Eia, Martyr Stephane

Fifteenth Century.

Eia, Martyr Stephane
Pray for us, we pray to thee.
To this martyr praise be given,
Qui triumphavit hodie,
And did gain the bliss of heaven,
Dono cœlestis gratiæ.
Stonëd he was with stonës great,
Fervore gentis impiæ.
Then saw he Christ set on His seat
Innixum Patris dextere.
Thou prayest Christ for thine enemies,
O martyr invictissime!
Then pray for us that high Justice
Ut nos purget a crimine. Amen.

Pray for us that we savèd be, Protomartyr Stephane

Before 1529.

In this vale of wretchedness,
Yprovëd was thy meekness,
Where thou art in joy and bliss,
Circumfultus undique.

With faith all armed in field to fight
Sad thou stoodest as God's [own] knight,
Teaching the people, of God His might,
O facies plena gracie!

Before the tyrant thou wert brought,
Strokes of pain thou dreadedst nought,
God was with thee in all thy thought,
Spes eterne glorie.

With sinful wretches thou were take,
Thy faith thou wouldest not forsake,
But rather to die for Godës sake,
Circumfuso sanguine.

Saint Stephen was a Clerk[1]

Fifteenth Century.

SAINT Stephen was a clerk in King Herod's hall,
And served him of bread and cloth, as ever king befall.

Stephen out of kitchen came with boar's head in [his] hand,
He saw a star [that] was fair and bright over Bethlehem stand.

He cast adown the boar's head and went into the hall:
" I forsake thee, King Herod, and thy workës all."

" I forsake thee, King Herod, and thy workës all;
There is a child in Bethlehem born is better than we all."

" What aileth thee, Stephen, what is thee befall?
Lacketh thee either meat or drink in King Herod's hall?"

[1] See note.

" Lacketh me neither meat nor drink in King Herod's hall,
There is a child in Bethlehem born is better than we all."

" What aileth thee, Stephen, art thou mad, or thou ginnest
to brede [1] ?
Lacketh thee either gold or fee or any richë weed ? "

" Lacketh me neither gold nor fee, nor no richë weed,
There is a child in Bethlehem born shall help us at our need."

" That is all so sooth, Stephen, all so sooth ywis,
As this capon crow [it] shall that lieth here in my dish."

That word was not so soonë said, that word in that hall,
The capon crew, *Christus natus est*, among the lordës all.

" Riseth up my tormentors, by twos and all by one,
And leadeth Stephen out of this town, and stoneth him with
stone."

Took [they then] Stephen and stoned him in the way,
Therefore is his even on Christës own day.

Now sing we, both all and some :
Lapidaverunt Stephanum

Before 1536.

WHEN Saint Stephen was at Jerusalem,
Godës laws he loved to learn,
That made the Jews to cry so clear and clean,
Lapidaverunt Stephanum.
Now sing we, both all and some :
Lapidaverunt Stephanum.

[1] Rave.

The Jews that were both false and fell,
Against Saint Stephen they were cruel,
Him to slay they made great yell,
And lapidaverunt Stephanum.
Now sing we, both all and some:
Lapidaverunt Stephanum.

They pullëd him without the town,
And then he meekly kneelëd down,
While the Jews cracked his crown,
Quia lapidaverunt Stephanum.
Now sing we, both all and some:
Lapidaverunt Stephanum.

Great stones and bones at him they cast,
Veins and bones of him they brast,[1]
And they killed him at the last,
Quia lapidaverunt Stephanum.
Now sing we both all and some:
Lapidaverunt Stephanum.

Pray we all that now be here,
Unto Saint Stephen, that martyr clear,
To save us all from the fiendës fear.
Lapidaverunt Stephanum.
Now sing we both all and some:
Lapidaverunt Stephanum.

[1] Burst.

Pray for us to the Prince of peace,
Amice Christi, Johannes[1]

Before 1529.

To thee now, Christ's dear darling,
That wert maiden[2] both old and ying,
My heart is set a song to sing,
Amice Christi, Johannes.

For thou wert so clean a maid,
The secrets of heaven were to thee said
When on Christ's breast thou wert laid,
Amice Christi, Johannes.

When Christ before Pilate was brought,
Thou, clean of heart, forsook Him nought,
To die with Him was all thy thought,
Amice Christi, Johannes.

Christ's mother thou tookest home with thee
Maiden, a maiden's friend to be,
Thou be our help, we pray to thee,
Amice Christi, Johannes.

Pray for us to the Trinity,
Johannes, Christi care

Before 1536.

Thou dearest disciple of Jesu Christ,
Most best belovëd and best betrust,[3]
Which at his Last Supper did lie on his breast,
Sacra fluenta potare.
Pray for us to the Trinity,
Johannes, Christi care!

[1] In another version the third person is used throughout.
[2] Bachelor. [3] Trusted.

As [He] in His Passion to His dear mother,
Took thee for her keeper, her son and His brother,
Pray that our hearts may most of all other
Jesum semper amare.
Pray for us to the Trinity,
Johannes, Christi care!

And as thou the strong venom which two men had slain,
Drank (thou) without hurt, and raised them again,
Pray that the venom of sin may us not pain,
Non poterit alligare.
Pray for us to the Trinity,
Johannes, Christi care!

As thou the two men their treasure did restore,
That had forsaken and mournëd therefore,
Pray that we may false riches forsake for evermore,
Celis tesaurizare.
Pray for us to the Trinity,
Johannes, Christi care!

And pray that we may have such grace,
Here so to mourn for our trespass,
That we may stand sicker [1] before Christ's face,
Cum venerit judicare.
Pray for us to the Trinity,
Johannes, Christi care!

[1] Secure. *Scotch,* sicker.

Worship we this holy day,
That all Innocents for us pray

Before 1529.

HEROD that was both wild and wode,
Full much he shed of Christian blood,
To slay that Child so meek of mood,
That Mary bare, that clean may.

Mary with Jesu forth yfraught,[1]
As the angel her taught,
To flee the land till it were sought,
To Egypt [2] she took her way.

Herod slew with pride and sin
Thousands of two year and within;
The body of Christ he thought to win
And to destroy the Christian fay.[3]

Now Jesus that didst die for us on the Rood,
And didst christen innocents in their blood,
By the prayer of Thy mother good,
Bring us to bliss that lasteth ay.

Psallite gaudentes,
Infantum festa colentes

Before 1529.

WHEN God was born of Mary free,
Herod, the king of Galilee,
Was moved to malice by kingës three
Munera portantes,
Regem natum venerantes.

[1] Laden. [2] *Text:* Epytte. [3] Faith.

Herod sent for men armed bright
To seek and slay the King of light;
The blessed Child drew fro Herod's might,
Armati sunt perimentes.

A, a, a, a,
Nunc gaudet ecclesia

Fifteenth Century.

LISTENETH, lordings, both great and small,
I shall you tell a wonder tale,
How Holy Church was brought in bale,
Cum magna injuria.

The greatest clerk in all this land,
Thomas of Canterbury, I understand,
Slain he was by wicked hand,
Demonis[1] *potencia.*

Knights camen fro Henry[2] king,
Wicked men, without leasing,[3]
There they diden a wonder thing,
Ferventes insania.[4]

They sought him all about,
Within the palace and without;
Of Jesu Christ had they no doubt,[5]
In sua malicia.

They opened their mouths wonder wide,
To Thomas they spaken mickle pride,
"Traitor, here, thou shalt abide,
Ferens mortis tedia."

[1] *Another reading:* malorum. [2] *Elsewhere,* Harry *and* Hendry.
[3] Lie, *i.e.* truly. [4] *Elsewhere:* Per regis imperia. [5] Fear.

Thomas answered with mildë cheer,
"If ye will me slay in this manner,
Let them pass, all that are here,
Sine contumel[i]a."

Beforn his altar he kneeled adown,
There they began to pare his crown;
They stirred the brainës up so down,[1]
Optans celi gaudia.

The tormentors about [they] start,
With deadly wounds they gan him hurt;
Thomas died in Mother-Church,
Pergens ad celestia.

Mother, clerk, widow, and wife,
Worship ye Thomas in all your life;
For fifty-two points [2] he lost his life,
Contra regis consilia.

[1] Upside down. [2] The Constitutions of Clarendon, 1164.

APPENDIX I[1]

LATIN, ANGLO-NORMAN, AND FRENCH CAROLS

Ecce quod Natura

Ecce quod natura
Mutat sua jura,
Virgo parit pura
  Dei Filium.

Ecce novum gaudium,
  Ecce novum mirum,
Virgo parit filium,
  Que non novit virum;
  Sed ut pirus pirum
  Gleba fert saphirum,
    Dei Filium.

Mundum Deus flebilem
  Videns in ruina,
Rosam dilectabilem
  Produxit de spina,
  Produxit de spina,
  Que celi regina
  Nostra medicina
Et salus hominum.

[1] See note.

Nequivit Divinitas
Plus humilimi;
Nec nostra fragilitas
Magis exaltari,
Magis exaltari,
Quam celo locari,
Deo coequari,
Per conjugina.

Seignors, Ore Entendez à Nus

Early Thirteenth Century.

Seignors, ore entendez à nus,
De loinz sumes venuz à wous,
Pur quere Noel;
Car l'em nus dit que en cest hostel
Soleit tenir sa feste anuel,
Ahi, cest jur.
Deu doint à tuz icels joie d'amurs,
Qui à Danz Noel ferunt honors!

Seignors, jo vus dis por veir,
Ke Danz Noel ne velt aveir
Si joie non;
E repleni sa maison
De payn, de char, e de peison,
Por faire honor.
Deu doint à tuz cels joie d'amurs,
Qui à Danz Noel ferunt honors!

Seignors, il est crié en l'ost,
Que cil qui despent bien, e tost,
E largement,

E fet les granz honors sovent,
Deu li duble quanque il despent,
Por faire henor.
Deu doint à tuz icels joie d'amours,
Qui à Danz Noel ferunt honors!

Seignors, escriez les malveis,
Car vuz nel les troverez jameis,
De bone part:
Botun, batun, ferun, groinard,
Car tot dis a le quer cunard
Por faire henor.
Deu doint à tuz icels joie d'amours,
Qui à Danz Noel ferunt honors!

Noel beyt bien li vin Engleis,
E li Gascoin, e li Franceys,
E l'Angevin;
Noel fait beivere son veisin,
Si qu'il se dort, le chief enclin,
Sovent le jor.
Deu doint à tuz cels joie d'amours,
Qui à Danz Noel ferunt honors!

Seignors, jo vus di par Noel,
E par li sires de cest hostel,
Car bevez ben;
E jo primes beverai le men,
E pois après chescon le soen,
Par mon conseil;
Si jo vus di trestoz, "Wesseyl!"
Dehaiz eit qui ne dirra, "Drincheyl!"

Anglo-Norman Carol

Translated by F. Douce.

Lordings, listen to our lay—
We have come from far away
To seek Christmas;
In this mansion we are told
He his yearly feast doth hold;
'Tis to-day!
May joy come from God above,
To all those who Christmas love.

Lordings, I now tell you true,
Christmas bringeth unto you
Only mirth;
His house he fills with many a dish
Of bread and meat and also fish,
To grace the day.
May joy come from God above,
To all those who Christmas love.

Lordings, through our army's band
They say—who spends with open hand
Free and fast,
And oft regales his many friends—
God gives him double what he spends,
To grace the day.
May joy come from God above,
To all those who Christmas love.

Lordings, wicked men eschew,
In them never shall you view
Aught that's good;

Cowards are the rabble rout,
Kick and beat the grumblers out,
To grace the day.
May joy come from God above,
To all those who Christmas love.

To English ale and Gascon wine,
And French, doth Christmas much incline—
And Anjou's, too ;
He makes his neighbour freely drink,
So that in sleep his head doth sink
Often by day.
May joy come from God above,
To all those who Christmas love.

Lords, by Christmas and the host
Of this mansion hear my toast—
Drink it well—
Each must drain his cup of wine,
And I the first will toss off mine :
Thus I advise.
Here then I bid you all *Wassail*,
Cursed be he who will not say, *Drinkhail*.
May joy come from God above,
To all those who Christmas love.

Célébrons la Naissance

Late Sixteenth Century.

CÉLÉBRONS la Naissance
Nostri Salvatoris,
Qui fait la complaisance
Dei sui Patris ;

Cet Enfan tout aimable,
In nocte media
Est né dans une étable
De casta Maria.
Cette heureuse nouvelle
Olim pastoribus
Par un ange fidelle
Fuit nunciatus,
Leur disant, " Laissez paître
In agro viridi,
Venez voir notre Maître,
Filiumque Dei."
A cette voix céleste
Omnes hi pastores,
D'un air doux et modeste,
Et multum gaudentes,
Incontinent marchèrent
Relicto pecore ;
Tous ensemble arrivèrent
In Bethlem Judæ.
Le premier qu'ils trouvèrent
Intrantes stabulum,
Fut Joseph, ce bon père,
Senio confectum,
Qui d'ardeur nompareille,
It obviam illis,
Les reçoit, les accueille
Expansis brachiis.
Il fait à tous caresse,
Et in præsepio
Fait voir plein d'alégresse
Matrem cum Filio ;

Ces bergers s'étonnèrent
Intuentes Eum,
Que les anges révèrent
Pannis involutum.
Lorsqu'ils se prosternèrent
Cum reverentia,
Et tous ils adorèrent,
Pietate summa,
Ce Sauveur tout aimable
Qui homo factus est,
Et qui dans une étable
Nasci dignatus est,
D'un cœur humble et sincère,
Suis muneribus,
Donnèrent à la mère
Et Filio ejus
Des marques de tendresse ;
Atque his peractis,
Font voir leur alégresse
Hymnis et canticis.
Mille esprits angéliques
Juncti pastoribus
Chantent dans leur musique :
" *Puer nobis natus ;*
Au Dieu par qui vous sommes,
Gloria in excelsis,
Et la paix soit aux hommes
Bonæ voluntatis ! "
Jamais pareilles fêtes !
Judicio omnium,
Même jusques aux bêtes
Testantur gaudium.

Enfin cette Naissance
Cunctis creaturis
Donne rejouissance,
Et replet gaudiis.
Qu'on ne soit insensible,
Adeamus omnes,
Ce Dieu rendu passible
Propter nos mortales,
Et tous de compagnie
Exoramus Eum,
Qu'a la fin de la vie
Dei regnum beatum.

APPENDIX II[1]

CAROLS NOT RELATED TO CHRISTMAS

A Carol of Hunting[2]

1521.

As I came by a green forest-side
I met with a forester that bade me abide,
With "Hey go bet,[3] hey go bet, hey go howe!"
Underneath a tree I did me set,
And with a great hart anon I met.
I bad let slip, and said, "Hey go bet!"
With "Hey go bet, hey go bet, howe!"
I had not stood there but a while,
For the maintenance of a mile,
There came a great hart, without guile:
"There he goeth, there he goeth, hey go howe!
We shall have game and sport ynow."
Talbot my hound with a merry taste
All about the green wood he gan cast.
I took my horn and blew him a blast,
With "Tro-ro-ro-ro, tro-ro-ro-ro!"
With "Hey go bet, hey go bet, hey go howe!
There he goeth, there he goeth, hey go howe!
We shall have sport and game ynow!"

[1] See Note. [2] *Christmas Carolles* (Wynkyn de Worde).
[3] Better or beat? Hey go bet *is a hunting cry.*

My Love that Mourneth for Me[1]

Temp. Henry VIII. John Gwynneth.

AND I mankind
Have not in mind,
  My love that mourneth for me, for me.
Who is my love
But God above
  That born was of Mary?

And on the Rood
His precious blood
  He shed to make me free.
Whom should I prove
So true of love
  So gentle and courteous as He?

That King of bliss
My love He is
  That mourneth so sore for me,
. . . .
. . . .
. . . . . .

The Father His Son
From heaven sent down
  That born was of a maid;
The prophecy
Of Isay
  Fulfillëd He and said:

[1] See note.

"Behold, mankind,
Thy Maker most loving
  For thy love come to die.
What is thy mind
To be so unkind
  Sith I so mourn for thee, for thee?"

That virgin's Child,
Most meek and mild,
  Alonely for my sake,
His Father's will
For to fulfill
  He came great pains to take.

And suffered death
As Scripture saith,
  That we should savëd be,
On Good Friday,
Wherefore I say
  He mourned sore for me, for me.

Such pain and smart
As in His heart
  He suffered for mankind,
Can no man take
Nor mourning make
  So meekly for his friend.

The cruel Jews
Would not refuse
  To nail Him to a tree,
And with a dart
To pierce His heart
  Thus mourned He for me.

Now Christ Jesu,
Of love most true,
  Have mercy upon me;
I ask the grace
For my trespass
  That I have done to Thee.

For Thy sweet name,
Save me from shame
  And all adversity;
For Mary's sake,
To Thee me take
  And mourn no more for me.

The Rose of Ryse[1]

Fifteenth Century.

THE rose is the fairest flower of all,
That evermore was, or evermore shall,
  The rose of ryse.[2]
  Of all these flowers the rose bears prize.
The rose, it is the fairest flower,
The rose is sweetest of odour.

The rose in care is comforter,
The rose in sickness it is salver,[3]
  The rose so bright.
  In medicine it is most of might,
Witness these clerkës that be wise.
The rose is the flower most holden in prize.

[1] MS. 31,042, fol. 110b. See note. [2] On the branch. [3] Saviour.

Therefore methinks the fleur-de-lys
Shouldë worship the rose of ryse,
And be his thrall;
And so should other flowers all.
Many a knight with spear and lance,
Followed that rose to his pleasance.

When the rose betided a chance,
Then followed all the flowers of France
And changëd hue,
In pleasance of the rose so true.

[Incomplete.]

My Heart of Gold[1]

1546-52.

My heart of gold as true as steel,
As I me leanëd to a bough,
In faith, but if ye love me well—
Lord! So Robin lough.[2]

My lady went to Canterbury,
The saint[3] her help to be;
She met with Kate of Malmesbury:
"Why sleepest thou in an apple-tree?"
My heart of gold, &c.

Nine miles to Michaelmas,
Our dame began to brew.
Michael set his mare to grass.
Lord! so fast it snew.
My heart of gold, &c.

[1] Richard Kele's *Christmas Carols.* See note.
[2] Laughed.
[3] Thomas à Becket.

"For you, love, I brake my glass;
Your gown is furred with blue.
The devil is dead, for there I was,
Ywis, it is full true.
My heart of gold, &c.

And if ye sleep, the cock will crow;
True heart, think what I say.
Jackanapes will make a mow[1];
Look, who dare say him nay?
My heart of gold, &c.

I pray you, have me now in mind,
I tell you of the matter.
He blew his horn against the wind;
The cow goeth to the water.
My heart of gold, &c.

Yet I tell you mickle more:
The cat lieth in the cradle.
I pray you, keep true heart in store,
A penny for a ladle.
My heart of gold, &c.

I swear by St. Katherine of Kent,
The goose goeth to the green,
All our dog's tail is brent,
It is not as I ween.
My heart of gold, &c.

Tyrlery lorpin the laverock sang,
So merrily pipes the sparrow;
The cow brake loose, the rope ran home—
Sir, God give you Good-Morrow!
My heart of gold, &c.

[1] Face.

All under the Leaves, and the Leaves of Life[1]

Traditional.

All under the leaves, and the leaves of life,
I met with virgins seven,
And one of them was Mary mild,
Our Lord's mother of heaven.

" O what are you seeking, you seven fair maids,
All under the leaves of life ;
Come tell, come tell, what seek you
All under the leaves of life ? "

" We're seeking for no leaves, Thomas,[2]
But for a friend of thine,
We're seeking for sweet Jesus Christ,
To be our guide and thine ! "

" Go down, go down to yonder town
And sit in the gallery,
And there you'll see sweet Jesus Christ
Nailed to a big yew-tree ! "

So down they went to yonder town
As fast as foot could fall,
And many a grievous bitter tear
From the Virgin's eye did fall.

" O peace, mother, O peace, mother,
Your weeping doth me grieve ;
I must suffer this," he said,
" For Adam and for Eve."

[1] See note. [2] Doubting Thomas?

"O mother, take you John Evangelist
  All for to be your son,
And he will comfort you sometimes,
  Mother, as I have done."

"O come thou, John Evangelist,
  Thou'rt welcome unto me,
But more welcome my own dear Son
  Whom I nursed on my knee."

Then he laid his head on his right shoulder,
  Seeing death it struck him nigh,
"The holy Mother be with your soul,
  I die, mother dear, I die."

O the rose, the gentle rose,
  And the fennel that grows so green,
God give us grace in every place
  To pray for our king and queen.

Furthermore for our enemies all
  Our prayers they should be strong:
Amen, good Lord; your charity
  Is the ending of my song.

To-morrow shall be My Dancing Day

Traditional.

To-MORROW shall be my dancing day,
  I would my true love did so chance
To see the legend of my play,
  To call my true love to my dance.
    Sing, oh! my love, oh! my love, my love, my love,
    This have I done for my true love.

Then was I born of a virgin pure,
  Of her I took fleshly substance;
Thus was I knit to man's nature,
  To call my true love to my dance.
    Sing, oh! my love, oh! my love, my love, my love,
    This have I done for my true love.

In a manger laid and wrapped I was,
  So very poor, this was my chance,
Betwixt an ox and a silly poor ass,
  To call my true love to my dance.
    Sing, oh! my love, oh! my love, my love, my love,
    This have I done for my true love.

Then afterwards baptized I was,
  The Holy Ghost on me did glance,
My Father's voice heard from above,
  To call my true love to my dance.
    Sing, oh! my love, oh! my love, my love, my love,
    This have I done for my true love.

Into the desert I was led,
  Where I fasted without substance;
The devil bade me make stones my bread,
  To have me break my true love's dance.
    Sing, oh! my love, oh! my love, my love, my love,
    This have I done for my true love.

The Jews on me they make great suit,
  And with me made great variance,
Because they loved darkness rather than light,
  To call my true love to my dance.
    Sing, oh! my love, oh! my love, my love, my love,
    This have I done for my true love.

For thirty pence Judas me sold,
  His covetousness for to advance.
Mark whom I kiss, the same do hold,
  The same is he shall lead the dance.
    Sing, oh! my love, oh! my love, my love, my love,
    This have I done for my true love.

Before Pilate the Jews me brought,
  Where Barabbas had deliverance,
They scourged me and set me at nought,
  Judged me to die to lead the dance.
    Sing, oh! my love, oh! my love, my love, my love,
    This have I done for my true love.

Then on the Cross hanged I was,
  Where a spear to my heart did glance;
There issued forth both water and blood,
  To call my true love to my dance.
    Sing, oh! my love, oh! my love, my love, my love,
    This have I done for my true love.

Then down to hell I took my way
  For my true love's deliverance,
And rose again on the third day,
  Up to my true love and the dance.
    Sing, oh! my love, oh! my love, my love, my love,
    This have I done for my true love.

Then up to heaven I did ascend,
  Where now I dwell in sure substance,
On the right hand of God, that man
  May come into the general dance.
    Sing, oh! my love, oh! my love, my love, my love,
    This have I done for my true love.

NOTES

P. 3. *Virgo Rosa Virginum.* Carols in honour of the Virgin belong almost entirely to pre-Reformation times, and bear marks of ecclesiastical origin in their frequent use of refrains from the Latin hymns. I have included in this group all carols in which special appeal is made to Mary. Many of them are among the most exquisite in feeling and melody.

P. 4. *Driht.* The Anglo-Saxon word for *Lord*, the latest use of which quoted in the New English Dictionary is 1450.

P. 7. *M and A and R and I.* This is the better of two very similar versions.

P. 8. *There is no Rose*, &c. This is one of thirteen carols found in a Cambridge MS., T.C.C. o. 3, 58, part of which at least is attributed to John Dunstable of Henry VII.'s Chapel. It is quite uncertain whether he wrote the words as well as the music.

P. 9. *Of a rose*, &c. There are two versions, differing slightly.

P. 14. *Alma Redemptoris Mater.* This carol is found in several versions differing slightly. The music was perhaps written by Dunstable.

P. 19. *Before* 1529. Because it is found in the Fairfax MS., supposed to have belonged to Robert Fairfax of Henry VIII.'s Chapel, who died in that year.

P. 20. *A song upon*, &c. I have not come upon the original on which this carol is based. It is a type of poem very popular in the fifteenth century, the Vision, and relates itself in treament to the more elaborate carol on p. 174; but it stands, I think, alone in representing Mary as prophesying the event, and picturing herself as singing lullaby.

P. 24. "*Marvel not, Joseph,*" &c. This carol and the following seem to be unique. I have classified them in this group because, after all, Mary is the poet's theme, the use made of Joseph being merely an original way of emphasizing the subject.

P. 25. *Joseph being an Aged Man.* The vague resemblances between this carol and the preceding suggest that they sprang from the same source, more especially as this aspect of the subject does not seem to be treated elsewhere. The idea is distinctly mediæval, as is shown by the occurrence of a similar dialogue in the *Pageant of the Shearmen and Tailors* (Coventry Plays). The subject is illustrated in MS. 17,587 (British Museum) about 1300, fol. c., where Joseph seems to be sleeping "on a frame." The refrain "dearest dear" suggests that the carol may have been adapted from some love-song.

P. 28. *Ecce Ancilla Domini.* The group of carols embodying the single incident of the Annunciation is clearly marked, but less original than some of the others in that the texts keep fairly close to the Biblical narrative. Most of them were written before the Reformation.

P. 38. *The Conception of Christ.* This was probably written by John Wedderburn, whose name is especially associated with the Reformation in Scotland. Its interest lies chiefly in its introduction of a lullaby refrain into the Annunciation episode.

P. 41. *In Die Nativitatis.* In this group I have tried to set apart the carols which treat of the Nativity chiefly from the historic and dramatic side. They merge into the class in which emphasis is laid on the meaning of the Incarnation (*Mirabile Misterium*). As most carols on this theme touch upon both phases, it is difficult sometimes to say which aspect is the more emphatic, consequently how the poem is to be classed. From the generalized treatment of the subject, on the one hand, and, on the other, from the attempt in small compass to touch upon the chief features of the incident, these carols are among the least interesting.

P. 49. *Frankincense.* The abrupt conclusion hints that the carol is incomplete, while the lack of rhyme in the last line shows corruption of the text.

P. 53. *Make we Joy*, &c. This carol might better be printed in the form of short couplets, alternately English and Latin. Its sole interest lies in its macaronic character. It is evidently with intention that a Latin line follows a Latin, and an English an English, while the rhyme is between one of each.

P. 54. *Come to Bethlehem*, &c. These five lines seem to be quoted from another carol to the music of which the text actually printed is modelled. This is seemingly unique in its theme, which is a contrasting of the moods of Advent, Christmas, Lent, and

Easter, *i.e.* the alternate fasts and feasts, the sentiment being that the former could be well spared.

P. 54. *A tansy.* This was a herb-dish intended as a corrective for the fish-diet of Lent. Various recipes are given for its preparation. The following is taken from a book of cookery with the sub-title *The Good Housewive's Handmaid*, 1597. "Take all manner of herbs and the spawn of a pike or any other fish and blanched almonds and a few crumbs of bread and a little fair water and a pint of rosewater, and mingle all together, and make it not too thin, and fry it in oil, and so serve it in." The fish ingredient was often lacking.

P. 55. *The First Nowell*, &c. This traditional carol, apparently first printed by Sandys in 1833, is yet quite in the old spirit.

P. 57. *Out of the Orient*, &c. This unpublished carol, written evidently not long before 1613 belongs still to the old tradition, but lacks the ingenuousness of the earlier lyrics.

P. 58. *Falantidingdido.* I have not found this refrain elsewhere, nor is it in the New English Dictionary. Notwithstanding the apparent suggestion of the word *tiding*, it seems to be mere nonsense; and from the rhythm I incline to think that it was accented *Falántidíngdidó.*

P. 59. *O Jesu Parvule.* Beyond doubt the most original and beautiful of the carols are those which depart from the Scripture material, and present imaginary scenes from the childhood of Christ, by far the greater number being the lullabies. Their popularity is attested not only by their number but also by the many repetitions with only slight variations. It seems reasonably certain *a priori* that the lullaby carols were suggested by the representations of the *crêche* in the churches, or by the Nativity scenes in the religious drama of the time. Indeed, the carol on p. 76 is taken from a miracle play.

P. 59. *I Saw*, &c. The simplest of all the lullabies is probably the oldest. The MS. in which it is found was said by T. Martin of Palgrave to be in the writing of John Brackley, friar minor of Norwich, tutor of William Paston, Justice of Common Pleas, 1378–1444. Although Brackley was still alive in 1461, a memorandum by John Whyte attributes the songs in the manuscript to the time of Richard II. and Henry IV. The music is given with the words.

P. 59. *This Endernight*, &c. This carol exists in at least four versions of which Dr. Dyboski prints three (E.E.T.S., Extra

Series CI.), giving the variants of the fourth. They are all so obviously from the same original and differ so slightly that, in consideration of their length, I have ventured to use them all in making a translation that is in some sense a composite. The chief variations are :—

1. A star as bright as *any* day, with the corresponding long line : Lullay, by-by, *lully*, lullay.

2. My Son, my *Brother*, my *dear darling.*

3. Then spake the Child that was so ying, and thus methought *He* said.

4. I am known as Heaven-King, &c.

5. To me shall light.

6. Now, Jesu, my son, Heaven-King, &c.

7. The Lord of might.

8. *For* And then among But nevertheless, &c., *from stanza* 2.

9. Mary, mother, queen of bliss, methinketh it is no law
That I should go to the kings and they not to me draw.

10. Jesu, my Son, I pray Thee, say as Thou art to me dear.

11. *For* Yet more than this, &c., *read:*
Both rock thee still
And dance Thee theretill.

12. *For* And keep me, &c., *read:* And dance me now full oft.

13. Jesu, my Son, Heaven-King, if it be Thy will,
Grant Thou me mine asking, as reason would and skill.

14. *For* That child or man, &c., *read:*
Whatsoever they be,
That can and will be.

15. Last stanza omitted.

P. 68. *Mother white*, &c. This carol shows in about its simplest form the extension of the episode in which the Child replies. In some of the sixteenth-century carols it grows into a long prophetic narrative of Christ's life and death uttered by Himself in the cradle, usually combined with a lullaby refrain.

P. 78. *Shall I, mother*, &c. Although the refrain suggests that this carol belongs to the preceding group, the narrative is entirely in the past, and Mary's part is wholly submerged.

P. 84. *The Holy Well.* This carol and the three following belong to a mass of traditions such as appear in the *Vita Christi* (MS. 29,434, *circa* 1400, in the British Museum), of which seemingly only these few have survived, at least in carol form. In an eighteenth-century broadside edition this poem is described as "a very ancient carol," and indeed, in spirit, as Mr. Bullen observes, it seems to be as old as the fifteenth century. Moreover, in the *Vita Christi* (fol. 56, 61) we have illustrations of Christ at a well with other children, which may refer to this or a similar legend.

P. 86. *The Bitter Withy*, or *The Withies*. This version of the preceding was sung in Herefordshire as late as 1888 (cf. *Notes and Queries*, tenth series, iv. pp. 84–85) by an old man who had learned it from his grandmother. It is noteworthy for the change of attitude; in the preceding carol it is Mary that is vindictive, in this the Christ-Child Himself. In the *Vita Christi* (fol. 64b) is a picture of three children in a river and Christ on the bank, which seems to illustrate this episode. The beating of the Child is said to be represented in a fresco at Lucca.

P. 87. *Three jolly jerdins*. The word *jerdin* seems to be unknown. It may have been corrupted from *virgins* to make alliteration, but the children were apparently boys.

P. 88. *The Cherry-Tree Carol*. Not having the numerous forms of this popular carol before me, I have followed Mr. Bullen in his eclectic version. The antiquity of the episode upon which it is based is shown by its occurrence in one of the Coventry plays. The scene is as follows:—

Mary. Ah, my sweet husband, will ye tell to me
What tree is yon standing upon yon hill?
Joseph. Forsooth, Mary, it is cleped a cherry-tree.
In time of year ye might feed you thereon your fill.
Mary. Turn again, husband, and behold yon tree,
How that it bloometh now so sweetly.
Joseph. Come on, Mary, that we were at yon city,
Or else we may be blamed, I tell you lightly.
Mary. Now, my spouse, I pray you to behold
How the cherries grow upon yon tree;
For to have thereof right fain I would,
An it pleased you to labour so much for me.
Joseph. Your desire to fulfil I shall assay sickerly.
Ow, to pluck you of these cherries it is a work wild,
For the tree is so high it will not be lightly;
Therefore let him pluck you cherries, begot you with child.
Mary. Now, good Lord, I pray Thee, grant me this boon,
To have of these cherries, if it be your will.

Now I thank it God, this tree boweth to me down,
I may now gather enow and eat my fill.
Joseph. Ow, I know well I have offended my God in Trinity,
Speaking to my spouse these unkind words;
For now I believe that my spouse beareth the King's Son of bliss, &c.

P. 91. *The Carnal and the Crane.* There is evidence of long tradition in the corruption of the text of this carol. It falls into two distinct sections: a generalised account of the Nativity, and a detailed account of the Flight into Egypt. Notwithstanding the disproportion of parts, there is no special reason for holding that they ever existed separately. The device of a theological discussion between two birds is a sufficiently mediæval introduction to a legend which was evidently popular in the fifteenth century, if we may judge from its frequent appearance as an illustration in *Books of Hours* of that period (cf. MSS. 17,280, 202b; 25,695, 114; 20,694, 65 in the British Museum. Doubtless there are many others). The incident of the "lovely lion" appears in the *Vita Christi*, MS. 29,434.

P. 96. *Gloria in Excelsis Deo.* With the exception of the three- or four-part song in the *Secunda Pastorum* (Towneley Plays), which I have included because of its general resemblance to the others, no shepherd carol has survived of a date earlier than the sixteenth century. However, the popularity of this aspect of the Nativity was very great during the late sixteenth and early seventeenth centuries, no doubt under the influence of the pastoral poetry which was then so fashionable. Many of these later compositions, often by well-known writers, are not true carols at all and are therefore relegated to Appendix III.

The shepherd carols show very great diversity of treatment and of merit.

P. 99. *As I rode*, &c. Apparently this is only another version of the preceding.

P. 99. *The Jolly Shepherd Wat.* This most realistic picture of the sixteenth-century shepherd suggests the similar handling of the theme in the mystery plays. See especially the *Secunda Pastorum,* where the homely gifts are a bob of cherries, a bird, and a ball, and the *Pageant of the Shearmen and the Tailors*, where a pipe, a hat, and mittens are offered. In the carol it is a pipe, scrip, tar-box, and skirt. Altogether, the poem reads very much like a short lyrical account of such a scene, and the phrase "Joseph with the round cape" suggests that the author had a mental image derived either from the stage or from some picture.

P. 110. *Reges de Saba Venient.* The Adoration of the Magi was one of the most popular subjects for pictorial and dramatic representation in the Middle Ages; but carols on the theme are few, elaborate, and not especially good. The first two carols are versions of the same to the end of the eleventh stanza; then the second, with some confusions, appends the Slaughter of the Innocents.

P. 114. *Us.* Apparently the Kings are speaking. It would seem as if a stanza has been lost in which they began to relate their journey.

P. 115. *Into Bethlehem,* &c. These lines seem to be misplaced. They fit in between the seventh and eighth stanzas, pp. 113–14.

P. 115. *Sun in glass.* Cf. p. 184. In this case the allusion seems to be to a burning-glass (cf. a beautiful illumination showing one in MS. 14 E 1, fol. 3, fifteenth century); in the second reference the idea may be the same, or it may allude to the transmission of light through glass without injuring the glass.

P. 121. *Nunc gaudet Ecclesia.* The first two carols in this group name the Saints' days kept at Christmas. Of these St. Stephen's Day, now Boxing Day, seems to have been most celebrated. Cf. p. 221–22, where Stephen is already invoked in connection with terms that suggest the custom of asking for "boxes."

The carols in this group are of very unequal merit.

P. 121. *Thou merry man.* An allusion to the personification of the season, doubtless as a part of the mumming practices. Cf. *Dan Noel* and *Sir Christmas.*

P. 123. *St. Stephen was a Clerk.* The central episode of this very quaint carol (cf. *The Carnal and the Crane*, p. 91, where the Magi bring the news) was related about 1200 by Vincent of Beauvais, who, however, tells it of two men at a dinner-table, one of whom, carving a fowl, said that he would do it so thoroughly that not Peter nor our Lord Himself could put it together again. Whereupon the cock was feathered and crowed, and both men became lepers.

A similar idea is illustrated in a print at the head of a carol-sheet published in 1701. It shows the stable at Bethlehem, the animals being represented with Latin inscriptions coming from their mouths as follows:—The cock: "Christus natus est." The raven: "Quando?" The cow: "Hac nocte." The ox: "Ubi?" The sheep: "Bethlehem."

P. 140. *My Love that Mourneth for Me.* This is an Easter carol obviously adapted from some earlier love-song. John Gwynneth was one of the Gentlemen of the Chapel to Henry VIII.

P. 142. *The Rose of Ryse.* Although this incomplete poem is distinctly labelled in the margin in a contemporary hand "A Christmas Carol," it seems to be rather political, alluding to the Tudor rose and the fleur-de-lys of France.

P. 143. *My Heart of Gold.* This is simply a nonsense rhyme or medley.

P. 145. *All under the Leaves,* &c. This is a traditional carol, which in spirit relates itself to the mystery plays of the Passion; but it has nothing to do with Christmas.

P. 146. *To-morrow shall be my Dancing-Day.* This traditional carol is perhaps a transformed love-song.

PART II

CAROLS OF THE DIVINE MYSTERY

Salve Regina

MIRABILE MISTERIUM

Mirabile misterium ![1]
The Son of God is man become

Fifteenth Century.

A MARVELOUS thing I have mused in my mind,
How that Veritas sprang right of the ground,
And Justicia, for all mankind,
From heaven to earth he came adown.
Mirabile misterium !
The Son of God is man become.

Then Mary, that merciful may,
Seeing man damned for his trespass
Hath sent down Sapientia, the sooth to say ;
Man is redeemed and brought to grace.
Mirabile misterium !
The Son of God is man become.

Celestial citizens, for us that you pray
To Him that is both Alpha and O,
That we may be savëd on Doomsday,
And brought to that bliss He bought us to !
Mirabile misterium !
The Son of God is man become.

[1] MS. Lansdowne 379, fol. 83.

The Flower of Jesse

About 1426. John Awdlay?

THERE is a Flower sprung of a tree,
The root thereof is called Jesse;
A Flower of price,
There is none such in Paradise!

This Flower is fair and fresh of hue;
It fadeth never, but ever is new;
The blissful branch this Flower on grew
Was Mary mild that bare Jesu.
A Flower of grace,
Against all sorrow it is solace!

The seed hereof was God's command,[1]
That God Himself sowed with His hand
In Bethlehem, in that holy land;
Amidst her harbour there he [2] her found.
This blissful Flower
Sprang never but in Mary's bower.

When Gabriel this maiden met,
With "Ave Maria" he her gret; [3]
Between them two this Flower was set,
And kept [It] was, no man shall wit;
But on a day
In Bethlehem It gan spread and spray.

[1] *Text:* Godes sond. [2] The angel. [3] Greeted.

When that Flower began to spread,
And His blossom forth He led,[1]
Rich and poor in every stead,[2]
They marvelled how this Flower might spread,
    And kinges three
  That blissful Flower came to see.

Angels there came out of their tower
To look upon this freshly Flower,
How fair He was in His colour,
And how sweet in His savour,
    And to behold
  How such a Flower might spring in gold!

Of lily, of rose of ryse,[3]
Of primrose, and of fleur-de-lys,
Of all the flowers at my device,
That Flower of Jesse yet bears the price
    As most of heal,
  To slake our sorrows every deal.

I pray thee, flowers of this countree,
Wherever ye go, wherever ye be,
Hold up the Flower of good Jesse,
For your freshness and your beauty,
    As fairest of all,
  And ever was and ever shall.

[1] *Text:* to brede, *i.e.* to flourish. [2] *Text:* of . . . lede.
[3] Branch.

O Flos de Jesse Virgula

Fifteenth Century.

O Flos de Jesse virgula
Laus Tibi sit gloria.

ADAM our father was in bliss,
And for an apple of little price,
He lost the bliss of Paradise,
Pro sua superbia.

And all that ever of him came
The right way to hellë nam,[1]
Both Isaac and Abraham,
Teste prophecia.

Then these prophets preached aforn,[2]
That a Child should be born
To buy what Adam had forlorn,
Sua morte propria.

Moses first in his law told
A Child there should be born so bold
To buy again what Adam sold,
Sua nocte pessima.

Isaac,[3] without leasing,
Prophesied in his preaching,
Of Jesse's root a Flower should spring
De virgine purica.

[1] Took. [2] Before. [3] *For* Isaiah.

Jeremy that was so ying,
Prophesied of His coming,
That is very Lord and King,
Summi Patris gracia.

Furthermore, as I you tell,
Then prophesied Daniel
Of His coming he gan spell,
Gentibus in Judæa.

When time came of God Almight,
That would bring mankind to right,
In a maiden He gan light,
Que vocatur Maria.

Now is He born, that blissful Child,
Of Mary mother, maiden mild;
Fro the fiend He us shield,
Qui creavit omnia.

Pray we to Him with all our mind,
That hath madë all mankind,
He bring us allë to good end,
In die novissima.

Adam Lay Ybounden

Fifteenth Century.

ADAM lay ybounden,
Bounden in a bond;
Four thousand winter
Thought he not too long.

And all was for an apple,
  An apple that he took,
As clerkës finden written
  In their book.
Nor had the apple taken been,
  The apple taken been,
Then had never our Lady
  A-been heaven's queen.
Blessed be the time
  That apple taken was!
Therefore we may singen
  Deo gracias!

All that 'lieve[1] in Christian lay,
Worship every Christmas day

Fifteenth Century.

A MAN[2] was the first guilt,
And therefore he was spilt;[3]
The prophecy was never [fulfilled],[4]
    Till on the Christmas day.

The first day that lily sprung,
Jesus Christ be us among,
Ever we thought it was too long,
    Till on the Christmas day.

It was dark, it was dim,
For men that livëd in great sin,
Lucifer was us all within,
    Till on the Christmas day.

[1] Believe.
[2] O' man, *i.e.* Of man.
[3] Destroyed.
[4] *Text repeats* spilt.

There was weeping, there was woe,
For every man to hell gan go.
It was little merry so,[1]
Till on the Christmas day.

Out of your Sleep Arise and Wake

About 1450.

Nowell, nowell, nowell, nowell, nowell, nowell.

Out of your sleep arise and wake,
For God mankind now hath ytake,
All of a maid without any make[2];
Of all women she beareth the bell.
Nowell.

And through a maiden fair and wise
Now man is made of full great price;
Now angels kneelen to man's service;
And at this time all this befell.
Nowell.

Now man is brighter than the sun;
Now man in heaven on high shall wone;[3]
Blessed be God, this game is begun,
And His mother empress of hell.
Nowell.

That ever was thrall, now is he free;
That ever was small, now great is she;
Now shall God deem both thee and me
Unto His bliss, if we do well.
Nowell.

[1] *Text:* tho=then. [2] Mate. [3] Dwell.

Now man may to heaven wend;
Now heaven and earth to him they bend;
He that was foe now is our friend.
This is no nay that I you tell.
Nowell.

Now blessed Brother, grant us grace,
At Doomësday to see Thy face,
And in Thy court to have a place,
That we may there sing *nowell.*
Nowell.

Exortum est in Love and Lysse

About 1450.

Nowell sing we, both all and some
Now Rex pacificus is come.

Exortum est in love and lysse.[1]
Now Christ His grace He gan us gysse,[2]
And with His body us bought to bliss,
Both all and some.

De Fructu ventris of Mary bright,
Both God and man in her alight,
Out of disease He did us dight,
Both all and some.

Puer natus to us was sent,
To bliss us bought, fro bale us blent,[3]
And else to woe we had ywent,
Both all and some.

[1] Delight. [2] Guide. [3] Turned.

Lux fulgebit with love and light,
In Mary mild His pennon pight,[1]
In her took kind with manly might,
Both all and some.

Gloria Tibi ay and bliss,
God unto His grace He us wysse,[2]
The rent of heaven that we not miss,
Both all and some.

What Tidings?

Fifteenth Century.

"What tidings bringest thou, messenger,
Of Christës birth this jolly day?"

A Babe is born of high nature,
The Prince of peace that ever shall be;
Of heaven and earth He hath the cure,[3]
His lordship is eternity.
Such wondrous tidings you may hear,
That man is made now Godës peer,
Whom sin had made but fiendës prey.

A wondrous thing doth now befall,
That King that formëd star and sun,
Heaven and earth and angels all,
Now in mankind is new begun.
Such wondrous tidings you may hear,
An infant of a single year,
That hath been ever and shall be aye.

[1] Placed. [2] Guide. [3] Charge.

That seemeth strange to us to see,
  This bird[1] that hath this Babe yborn,
And Lord conceived of high degree
  A maiden is and was beforn.
      Such wondrous tidings you may hear,
      That maiden and mother are one in fere,
        And she a lady of great array.

That loveliest gan greet her Child:
  "Hail, Son! Hail, Brother! Hail, Father dear!"
"Hail, Daughter!" He saith: "Hail, Sister. Hail,
    Mother mild!"
  This hailing was on quaint manner.
      Such wondrous tidings you may hear,
      That hailing was of so good cheer,
        That man his pain is turned to play.

Tidings, tidings that be true:[2] *Sorrow is past and joy doth renew*

Fifteenth Century.

WHEREAS Adam caused by sin
Our nature thus to be mortal,
    And that is true,
A maiden's Son doth now begin
For to repoise us from that fall,
    The name of Him is Christ Jesu.

Some of our kind hath had such grace
That since His birth they did Him see,
    And that is true,

[1] Lady. [2] MS. Lansdowne, 379, fol. 38.

Both Son and mother, face to face,
In the chief city called Jewry:
Both kings and shepherds, they it knew.

The prophets thereof were nothing dismayed
Of that tidings beforn that they had told,
And that is true;
For now it is fallen right as they said:
A maiden clean a king hath born;
For He is born to wear the purple hue.

This Babe to Us that now is Born

Fifteenth Century.

Now may we singen as it is
Quod puer natus est nobis.

THIS Babe to us that now is born,
Wonderful works He hath [y]wrought
He would not lose what was forlorn,
But boldly again it bought;
And thus it is
For sooth ywis,
He asketh nought but that is His.

This bargain lovëd He right well,
The price was high and bought full dear.
Who would suffer and for us feel
As did that Prince withouten peer?
And thus it is
For sooth ywis,
He asketh nought but that is His.

His ransom for us hath ypaid;
Good reason have we to be His.
Be mercy asked and He be prayed,
We may deserve the heavenly bliss.
And thus it is
For sooth ywis,
He asketh nought but that is His.

To some purpose God made man;
I trust well to salvation.
What was His blood that from Him ran
But fence against damnation?
And thus it is
For sooth ywis,
He asketh nought but that is His.

Almighty God in Trinity,
Thy mercy we pray with whole heart,
Thy mercy may all woe make flee
And dangerous dread from us to start.
And thus it is
For sooth ywis,
He asketh nought but that is His.

Now sing we with joy and bliss:
Puer natus est nobis

Before 1536.

MARY, flower of flowers all,
Hath born a child in an ox-stall,
That Lord and Prince is over us all;
Puer natus est nobis.

He was born on our lady,
Without sin of her body,
Godës own true Son truly;
Puer natus est nobis.

By an apple of a tree,
Bondmen all made were we,
That Child was born to make us free;
Puer natus est nobis.

That Child was done on the Rood,
With His flesh and with His blood,
For our help and for our good;
Puer natus est nobis.

The third day He rose and to heaven went,
Wit and wisdom He us sent,
For to keep His commandment;
Puer natus est nobis.

He shall come down at Doomësday,
With bloody woundës, I you say,
As He died on Good Friday;
Puer natus est nobis.

Now pray we to that heaven[ly] King,
To send us all His dear blessing,
Shrift and housel at our ending.
Puer natus est nobis.

This Day

About 1450.

An heavenly song, I dare well say,
Is sung on earth to man this day.

THIS is the song that ye shall hear,
God is come from His empire,
And is made man with high desire,
This day.

He took our kind all of a maid,
By ox and ass He was ylaid.
Now is fulfilled that Scripture said,
This day.

Ay I wonder this in my mind,
That He that all may loose and bind,
Would be laid by beasts unkind,
This day.

He is a lord and by nature
A maiden's breast He sucked full pure.
Heaven and earth be in His cure,
This day.

Now is Well and All Things Aright

Fifteenth Century.

Now is *well* [1] and all things aright,
And Christ is come as a true knight;
For our Brother is King of might,
The fiend to fleme [2] and all his.
Thus the fiend is put to flight,
And all his boast abated is.

[1] *A pun upon* Nowell.

[2] To put to flight.

Sithen it is, well [must] we do,
For there is none but one of two,
Heaven to get or heaven forego,
  Other mean none there is;
I counsel you, since it is so,
  That you well do to win you bliss.

Now is *well* and all is well,
  And right well, so have I bliss;
And sithen all things are so well,
  I rede [1] we do no more amiss.

Make we merry in this feast,
For verbum caro factum est

Fifteenth Century.

GODĒS Son for the love of man,
Flesh and blood of Mary He nam,[2]
As in the gospel saith Saint John,
    Verbum caro factum est.

Of joy and mirth now may we sing,
God with man is now dwelling,
Holy Writ maketh now shewing,
    Deus homo natus est.

God and man hath shewed His Child,
That hath us bought fro the devils wild;
Him to worship now be we mild,
    Congaudere mihi.

[1] Counsel. [2] Took.

This Child His mother ever more,
Maiden she was, after and before,
And so said the prophet in his lore,
Verbo prophesye.

As I Went through a Garden Green

Fifteenth Century.

As I went through a garden green,
I found an arbour made full new;
A fairer sight had I none seen,
On every tree sang a turtle true.
Therein a woman bright of hue,
She said in her song not least;
This was her carping as I knew:
Verbum caro factum est.

To her song then took I intent,
She said a song with voice clear:
. . . .
. . . .
"This Prince that is without a peer
Is born and lain between twain beast,
I sing as thou might hear:[1]
Verbum caro factum est."

In that wone[2] forth gan I wende,[3]
A seemly song then heard I tho,[4]
Of three shepherds that were full hend:[5]
"*Gloria in excelsis Deo.*"

[1] *Text:* lere=learn. [2] Abode. [3] *Text:* "winde." [4] Then. [5] Gentle; *text:* "hind."

I would not they had fared me fro,
  Well fast after them gan I haste;
They told me that they sungen so,
  For *verbum caro factum est.*

Yet furthermore in that frith [1]
  I saw three kingës come with crown,
I sped me fast to speak them with,
  And to those lords I kneelëd down.
The kings courteous to me gan sound,
  And saiden they would fare in haste;
"To Bedlem bower now are we bound,
  For *verbum caro factum est.*"

This is as much as for to say,
  As Godës Son become is flesh.
He was born this ilkë [2] day,
  A blissful way us for to wych.[3]
That may now, withouten miss,[4]
  Here I show both more and least,
For she was the cause ywis
  Of *verbum caro factum est.*

Godës Son become is flesh,
  That boot hath of all our bale,[5]
A blissful way us for to wych,
  That maid Him harboured in her hale [6]
She bore that Lovely in her Sale,[7]
  She held that Hend [8] within her breast;
With true tongue she told the tale
  For *verbum caro factum est.*

[1] Glade. [2] Very. [3] Show. [4] Without mistake. [5] Remedy for all our trouble. [6] Safe. [7] Body? [8] *Text:* Hind.

Verbum caro is to say
That Godës Son become is man;
He was born this ilkë day
To save us fro the fiend Sathan.
That may that is white as swan,
She fed that Lord upon her breast;
Therefore I sing you as I can,
Verbum caro factum est.

Jesu, as Thou art our Saviour

Fifteenth Century.

Jesu, Jesu, Jesu, Jesu,
Save us all through Thy virtue.

Jesu, as Thou art our Saviour
That Thou save us fro dolour!
Jesu is mine paramour.
Blessed be Thy name, Jesu.

Jesu was born of a may,
Upon Christëmas Day,
She was may beforn and ay,
Blessed be Thy name, Jesu.

Three kingës comen fro Segent,
To Jesu Christ they brought present.
Lord God Omnipotent,
Save us all through Thy virtue.

Jesu died and shed His blood
For all mankind upon the Rood;
He grant us grace of happës [1] good,
I beseech Thee, sweet Jesu.

Jesu, for Thy mother's sake,
Keep us fro the fiendës black;
Against Him that we may wake;
And save us all through Thy virtue.

Alleluia, alleluia

Fifteenth Century.

Now may we mirthës make,
For us Jesus manhood hath take, [2]
De virgine Maria,
Only for our sins' sake,
Alleluia.

The King of kings now forth is brought,
Of a maid that sinnëd nought,
Res miranda,
Neither in deed, neither in thought,
Alleluia.

The angel of counsel that day was born,
As propheciës said beforn,
Sol de stella,
For to save that [3] was forlorn, [4]
Alleluia.

[1] Good fortunes. [2] Taken. [3] What. [4] Lost.

Alleluia, alleluia, alleluia,
Alleluia, alleluia, alleluia,
Deo Patri sit gloria

Fifteenth Century.

Salvator mundi, Domine,
Father of heaven, blessed Thou be,
Thou greetest a maid with an avé,
Que vocatur Maria.

Adesto nunc propicius,
Thou sendest Thy Son, sweet Jesus,
Man to become for love of us,
Deo Patri sit gloria.

Ne mentem sompnus opprimat,
Betwixt an ox and an ass
Christ Himself born He was
De virgine Maria.

Te, Reformator sensuum,
Both little and mickle, and all and some,
Welcome the time that now is come,
Deo Patri sit gloria.

Gloria Tibi, Domine,
Three Persons in Trinity,
Blessed may They allë be,
Deo Patri sit gloria.

Alleluia, alleluia,
De virgine Maria

Fifteenth Century.

Salvator mundi, Domine,
Father of heaven, blessed Thou be,
And Thy Son that cometh of Thee,
De virgine Maria.

Adesto nunc propicius,
He sent His Son, sweet Jesus;
A man became for love of us,
De virgine Maria.

Te, Reformator sensuum,
Little and mickle, more and some,
Worship that Child that is come
De virgine Maria.

Gloria Tibi, Domine,
Three Persons in Trinity;
Worship that Child so free
De virgine Maria.

Te laudamus, Te Dominum
Confitemur, Te eternum

Temp. Henry VII. or VIII.

O BLESSED God in Trinity,
Great cause we have to bless Thy name,
That now wouldst send adown fro Thee
The Holy Ghost to stint [1] our blame.
Te Deum laudamus.

[1] Stop.

Sing we to God, Father Eternal,
That liketh, to tune with our nature,
The Son of Him Celestial
Man to be born, our souls to cure.[1]
Te Deum laudamus.

All the saints in heaven on high,
And all that be in earth also,
Give laud and thanks devotedly,
To God above and sing him to,
Te Deum laudamus.

Nowell, el, el, el, el, *I thank [it] a maiden every deal*

Fifteenth Century.

The first day when Christ was born,
There sprang a rose out of a thorn,
To save mankind that was forlorn;
I thank [it] a maiden every deal.

In an ox-stall the Child was found,
In poor clothing the Child was wound;
He suffered many a deadly wound;
I thank [it] a maiden every deal.

A garland of thorns on His head was set,
A sharp spear to His heart was smet;[2]
The Jews saiden, "Take Thee that!"
I thank [it] a maiden every deal.

1 God liketh His Son to be born man, to tune with our nature, for the saving of our souls.
2 Smitten.

The Jews did cry their parliament;
On the day of judgëment,
They were afeared they should be shent.[1]
I thank it a maiden every deal.

To the pillar He was bound,
To His heart a spear was stung;
For us He suffered a deadly wound.
I thank it a maiden every deal.

Blessed may Thou be, sweet Jesus,
Qui hodie natus es nobis

Before 1529. Richard Smert.[2]

By Thy birth, Thou blessed Lord,
Is made of variance now one accord;
Therefore we may sing[en] this:
Blessed may Thou be, sweet Jesus,
Qui hodie natus es nobis.

Upon this high [and] blessed day,
Jesu in His mother's arms lay,
Wherefore to Him let us all say:
Blessed may Thou be, sweet Jesus,
Qui hodie natus es nobis.

Jesu, Fili virginis,
Miserere nobis

Before 1529. Richard Smert.

Jesus, of a maid Thou wouldst be born,
To save mankind that was forlorn,
And all for our miss,[3]
Miserere nobis.

[1] Destroyed. [2] See note. [3] Sin.

Born Thou wert of Mary free,
And Thou didst die upon the Rood Tree,
And all for our miss,
Miserere nobis.

Jesu, Fili virginis,
Miserere nobis

Temp. Henry VII. or VIII.

Jesus, of a maid Thou wouldst be born,
To save mankind that was forlorn,
And all for our sins,
Miserere nobis.

Angels there were, mild of mood,
Sang to that sweet fode [1]
With joy and bliss.
Miserere nobis.

In a cratch [2] was that Child laid,
Both ox and ass with Him played,
With joy and bliss.
Miserere nobis.

Then for us He shed His blood,
And also He died on the Rood,
And for us ywis.
Miserere nobis.

And then to hell He took the way,
To ransom them that there[in] lay,
With joy and bliss.
Miserere nobis.

[1] Child. [2] Crib.

Jesu, Fili Dei,
Miserere me

Before 1529. John Trouluffe and Richard Smert.

GLORIOUS God in Trinity,
Well of man and [of] pity,
Thus cried the woman of Canaan-y,
Miserere me.

Thou came from heaven from Thy see,[1]
To this world a man to be;
Therefore I cry devoutly,
Miserere me.

As Thou hadst on her pity,
So I pray Thou have on me,
Glorious God in Trinity,
Miserere me.

To bliss God bring us, all and some,
Christe Redemptor omnium

Fifteenth Century.

IN Bethlehem, in that fair city,
A Child was born of our Lady,
Lord and prince that He should be,
A solis ortus cardine.

Children were slain [full] great plenty,
Jesus, for the love of Thee;
Let us never damnëd be,
Hostis Herodes impie.

[1] Estate.

He was born of our Lady,
Without stain of her body,
Godës Son that sitteth on high,
Iesu Salvator seculi.

As the sun shineth thorough the glass,
So Jesus in her body was;
To serve Him He gave us grace.
O lux beata trinitas!

Now is born our Lord Jesus,
That made merry all [of] us;
Be all merry in this house,
Exultet celum laudibus!

Into this world now is come Christe Redemptor omnium

Before 1536.

O WORTHY Lord and most of might,
Eterne rex altissime,
Thee to honour me thinketh right,
Iam lucis orto sidere.

As Thou art Lord of worthiness,
Conditor alme siderum,
All us to bring out of darkness,
Christe Redemptor omnium.

With beamës clear of righteousness,
Aurora lucis rutilat,
In joy thereof with all gladness,
Vox clara ecce intonat.

Now glorious Lord and worthy King,
Jesu Salvator seculi,
Grant us Thy bliss everlasting,
Summi Largitor premii!

Verbum Patris hodie processit ex virgine

Before 1536.

THE Son of the Father of heavenly bliss
Was born [on[1]] this day, I will not miss,
Man from thraldom to relieve and release,
Processit ex virgine.

He was born of a virgin pure,
Not knowing a man, as I you assure;
But all only by heavenly cure
Processit ex virgine.

Gabriel the angel met
Mary kneeling in her closet;
Now is fulfilled what said the prophet:
Processit ex virgine.

Man, be glad, thou hast a cause why
To thank our Lord God that is on high;
For thee to suffer and for to die,
Processit ex virgine.

[1] *Text:* as.

A blessed bird, as I you say,
That died and rose on Good Friday

Before 1536.

On Christës day, I understand,
An ear of wheat of a maid sprang,
Thirty winters on earth to stand,
To make us bread, all to His pay.[1]
A blessed bird, as I you say,
That died and rose on Good Friday.

This corn was reapen and laid to ground,
Full sore beaten and fastë bound
Unto a pillar with cordës round,
At His fingers' ends the blood ran out that day.
A blessed bird, as I you say,
That died and rose on Good Friday.

This corn was reapen with great envy
Upon the Mount of Calvary;
Token He showed on Shere-Thursday,
Maundy He gave to His disciples there.
A blessed bird, as I you say,
That died and rose on Good Friday.

Jesu upon His body the Cross bare;
Water and blood came from Him there;
This corn was scourged all in fere;
Till it waxed blood-red.
A blessed bird, as I you say,
That died and rose on Good Friday.

[1] Liking.

A crown of thorns set on His head,
And He was done on the Rood,
And beaten till His body was bloody-red;
Thus they beat Jesu, our debt to pay.
A blessed bird, as I you say,
That died and rose on Good Friday.

Now sing we, sing we: Gloria Tibi, Domine

Before 1536.

CHRIST keep us all, as He well can,
A solis ortus cardine;
For He is both God and Man,
Qui natus est de virgine.
Sing we, sing we: Gloria Tibi, Domine.

As He is Lord, both day and night,
Venter puelle baiulat,
So is Mary, mother of might,
Secreta que non noverat.
Sing we, sing we: Gloria Tibi, Domine.

The holy breast of chastity,
Verbo concepit Filium,
So brought before the Trinity,
Ut castytatis lyllyum.
Sing we, sing we: Gloria Tibi, Domine.

Between an ox and an ass
Enixa est puerpera;
In poor clothing clothed He was,
Qui regnat super ethera.
Sing we, sing we: Gloria Tibi, Domine.

Sing we all, for time it is:
Mary hath borne the Fleur-de-lys

Before 1536.

For His love that bought us all dear,
Listen, lordings, that be here,
And I well tell you in-fere,[1]
Whereof came the Fleur-de-lys.
Sing we all, for time it is:
Mary hath borne the Fleur-de-lys.

On Christmas night, when it was cold,
Our Lady lay among beastës bold,
And there she bare Jesù, Joseph told,
And thereof came the Fleur-de-lys.
Sing we all, for time it is:
Mary hath borne the Fleur-de-lys.

Of that beareth witness Saint John,
That it was of much renown;
Baptized he was in stream Jordan,
And thereof came the Fleur-de-lys.
Sing we all, for time it is:
Mary hath borne the Fleur-de-lys.

On Good Friday that Child was slain,
Beaten with scourges and all to-flayn;[2]
That day he suffered mickle pain;
And thereof came the Fleur-de-lys.
Sing we all, for time it is:
Mary hath borne the Fleur-de-lys.

[1] Together. [2] Flayed.

I pray you, be merry and sing with me
In worship of Christ's Nativity

Before 1536.

INTO this world, this day did come
Jesu Christ, both God and man,
Lord and Servant in one person,
Born of the blessed virgin Mary.
I pray you, be merry and sing with me
In worship of Christ's Nativity.

He that was rich, without any need,
Appeared in this world in right poor weed,
To make us that were poor indeed,
Rich without any need, truly.
I pray you, be merry and sing with me
In worship of Christ's Nativity.

A stable was His chamber; a cratch [1] was His bed;
He had not a pillow to lay under His head
With maiden's milk that babe was fed,
In poor clothes was lapped the Lord Almighty.
I pray you, be merry and sing with me
In worship of Christ's Nativity.

A noble lesson here is us taught,
To set all worldly riches at naught,
But pray we that we may be thither brought,
Where riches is everlastingly.
I pray you, be merry and sing with me
In worship of Christ's Nativity.

[1] Crib.

Sing we with mirth, joy and solace
In honour of this Christëmas

Before 1536.

GLORIOUS God had great pity,
How long man's soul in pain should be;
He sent His Son to make us free,
Which for man's sake,
Of a maiden pure,
Against nature,
Our flesh did take.
Sing we with mirth, joy and solace
In honour of this Christëmas!

In Bethlehem our Saviour,
Without food, in a manger
Was born—it was his pleasure—
Beastës among.
Angels heavenly
Made harmony
And joyful song.
Sing we with mirth, joy and solace
In honour of this Christëmas!

The eighth day he was circumcised,
Lest Moses' law should be despised;
A name to him they have devised,
Call him Jesus;
For Gabriel
His mother did tell
That it should be thus.
Sing we with mirth, joy and solace
In honour of this Christëmas.

A new-made star, more large and clear
Than other stars, then did appear.
Fro Chaldea the philosophers in fere
    Into Bethlehem it brought.
There it did stand
Still, till that they found
    Him that they sought.
        Sing we with mirth, joy and solace
        In honour of this Christëmas!

The kingës brought their offering,
Gold that betokeneth a worthy king,
Incense, priesthood; myrrh burying
    For his manhood.
The angel come
Bade them go home
    Not by Herod.
        Sing we with mirth, joy and solace
        In honour of this Christëmas!

Trust in God, man, and in none other;
Mistrust Him not, He is thy brother;
Thou hast a mediatrix of His mother.
    Sigh for thy sin,
Cry mercy,
He will not deny
    Thy soul to win.
        Sing we with mirth, joy and solace
        In honour of this Christëmas!

Of the Birth of Christ

1487–1568. Miles Coverdale.

Now blessed be Thou, Christ Jesu,
Thou art man born this is true;
The angels made a merry noise,
Yet have we more cause to rejoice,
Kirieleyson.

The blessed Son of God only,
In a crib full poor did lie,
With our poor flesh and our poor blood,
Was clothed that everlasting Good,
Kirieleyson.

He that made heaven and earth of nought,
In our flesh hath our health brought,
For our sake made He Himself full small,
That reigneth Lord and King over all,
Kirieleyson.

Eternal light doth now appear,
To the world both far and near,
It shineth full clear even at midnight,
Making us children of his light,
Kirieleyson.

The Lord Christ Jesus, God's Son dear,
Was a guest and a stranger here,
Us for to bring from misery,
That we might live eternally,
Kirieleyson.

Into this world right poor came He,
To make us rich in mercy,
Therefore would He our sins forgive,
That we with Him in heaven might live,
Kirieleyson.

All this did He for us freely,
For to declare His great mercy;
All christendom be merry therefore,
And give Him thanks ever more,
Kirieleyson.

Lully, lulley, lully, lulley,
The falcon hath borne my make[1] *away*[2]

Before 1536.

He bare him up, he bare him down,
He bare him into an orchard brown.

In that orchard there was an hall,
That was hangëd with purple and pall.

And in that hall there was a bed,
It was hangëd with gold so red.

And in that bed there lieth a knight,
His woundës bleeding, day and night.

By that bedside kneeleth a may,
And she weepeth both night and day.

And by that bedside there standeth a stone,
Corpus Christi written thereon.

[1] Mate.
[2] See note.

All Bells in Paradise [1]

Traditional.

OVER yonder's a park, which is newly begun,
All bells in Paradise, I heard them a-ring;
Which is silver on the outside and gold within,
And I love sweet Jesus above all thing.

And in that park there stands a hall,
All bells in Paradise I heard them a-ring;
Which is covered all over with purple and pall,
And I love sweet Jesus above all thing.

And in that hall there stands a bed,
All bells in Paradise I heard them a-ring;
Which is hung all round with silk curtains so red,
And I love sweet Jesus above all thing.

And in that bed there lies a knight,
All bells in Paradise I heard them a-ring;
Whose wounds they do bleed by day and by night,
And I love sweet Jesus above all thing.

At that bedside there lies a stone,
All bells in Paradise I heard them a-ring;
Which is our blessed Virgin Mary then kneeling on,
And I love sweet Jesus above all thing.

At that bed's foot there lies a hound,
All bells in Paradise I heard them a-ring;
Which is licking the blood as it daily runs down,
And I love sweet Jesus above all thing.

[1] See note.

At that bed's head there grows a thorn,
All bells in Paradise I heard them a-ring;
Which was never so blossomed since Christ was born,
And I love sweet Jesus above all thing.

Remember, O thou Man[1]

Before 1567.

REMEMBER, O thou man,
O thou man, O thou man!
Remember, O thou man!
Thy time is spent;
Remember, O thou man, how thou art dead
and gone,
And I did what I can, therefore repent;
Remember Adam's fall,
O thou man, O thou man!

Remember Adam's fall,
From heaven to hell;
Remember Adam's fall,
How we were condemned all,
In hell perpetual
Therefore to dwell,
Remember God's goodness,
O thou man, man, O thou man!

Remember God's goodness,
And His promise made,
Remember God's goodness,
How He sent His Son doubtless,
Our sins for to redress,
Be not afraid.

[1] Ravenscroft's *Melismata, Musical Phansies*, &c., 1611. See note.

The angels all did sing,
O thou man, O thou man!
The angels all did sing,
Upon the shepherds' hill.
The angels all did sing,
Praises to our heavenly king,
And peace to man living,
    With a good will.

The shepherds amazëd was,
O thou man, O thou man!
The shepherds amazëd was,
To hear the angels sing;
The shepherds amazëd was,
How it should come to pass,
That Christ our Messias,
    Should be our King.

To Bethlehem did they go,
O thou man, O thou man!
To Bethlehem did they go,
The shepherds three;
To Bethlehem did they go,
To see whe'er it were so or no,
Whether Christ were born or no,
    To set man free.

As the angels before did say,
O thou man, O thou man!
As the angels before did say,
So it came to pass;

As the angels before did say,
They found a babe where it lay,
In a manger wrapped in hay,
    So poor he was.

In Bethlehem he was born,
O thou man, O thou man!
In Bethlehem he was born,
For mankind's sake.
In Bethlehem he was born,
For us that were forlorn,
And therefore took no scorn,
    Our flesh to take.

Give thanks to God always,
O thou man, O thou man!
Give thanks to God always,
With heart most joyfully;
Give thanks to God always,
For this our happy day;
Let all men sing and say,
    Holy holy.

For Christmas Day

1584?–1659. T. Pestell.

FAIREST of morning lights, appear,
  Thou blest and gaudy day,
On which was born our Saviour dear;
  Arise and come away.

This day prevents His day of doom;
  His mercy now is nigh;
The mighty God of Love is come,
  The Dayspring from on high.

Behold, the great Creator makes
  Himself an house of clay,
A robe of virgin-flesh He takes
  Which He will wear for aye.

Hark, hark, the wise Eternal Word
  Like a weak infant cries;
In form of servant is the Lord,
  And God in cradle lies.

This wonder struck the world amazed,
  It shook the starry frame;
Squadrons of spirits stood and gazed,
  Then down in troops they came.

Glad shepherds ran to view this sight;
  A quire of angels sings;
And eastern sages with delight
  Adore this King of kings.

Christmas Day

1588-1667. George Wither.

As on the night before this happy morn,
  A blessed angel unto shepherds told,
Where (in a stable) He was poorly born,
  Whom nor the earth nor heaven of heavens can hold:
    Through Bethlehem rung
      This news at their return:
    Yea, angels sung
      That God with us was born;
And they made mirth because we should not mourn.

This angel-carol sing we, then,
To God on high all glory be,
For peace on earth bestoweth He,
And showeth favour unto men.

This favour Christ vouchsafed for our sake;
To buy us thrones, He in a manger lay,
Our weakness took, that we His strength might take;
And was disrobed that He might us array;
Our flesh He wore,
Our sin to wear away;
Our curse He bore,
That we escape it may;
And wept for us that we might sing for aye.
With angels, therefore, sing again,
To God on high all glory be;
For peace on earth bestoweth He,
And showeth favour unto men.

Born is the Babe [1]

Early Seventeenth Century.

Born is the Babe, the only Branch of Peace,
The sweet Messias, God's most holy Son,
Whose death our life, whose wounds our joys increase,
Who wrought our weal when all our hope was gone,
Whose grief our joy, whose lack relieved our loss,
Who cured our care by suffering on the Cross.

Born is the Lamb, the Sacrifice of Joy,
The Spotless Person, Ransom of our sin,

[1] MS. Additional 7790, fols. 6b, 7.

The sweet Samaritan that cured all annoy,
The Son (in) whom the Sire delighted in,
The Haven of Peace when worldly troubles toss,
Who cured our care by suffering on the Cross.

Born is the Shepherd careful of his sheep,
The Light of Glory bright of majesty,
The Father's Power who hath our sins in keep,
The very Beam of true Divinity,
Whom praise we still when worldly troubles toss,
Who cured our care by suffering on the Cross.

Sun of Righteousness [1]

1632.

All this night shrill chanticleer,
Day's proclaiming trumpeter,
Claps his wings and loudly cries,
"Mortals, mortals, wake and rise!
See a wonder
Heaven is under,
From the earth is risen a Sun
Shines all night though day be done.

Wake, O earth, wake everything,
Wake and hear the joy I bring,
Wake and joy; for all this night
Heaven and every twinkling light,
All amazing,
Still stand gazing,
Angels, powers and all that be,
Wake and joy this Sun to see.

[1] *A Handfull of Celestiall Flowers*, manuscrib'd by R. Cr. (Ralph Crane).

Hail, O Sun, O blessed Light,
Sent into the world by night,
Let thy rays and heavenly powers
Shine in this dark soul of ours;
For most duly
Thou art truly
God and man we do confess.
Hail, O Sun of Righteousness!"

The Moon Shone Bright; or, The Bellman

THE moon shone bright, and the stars gave a light,
A little before it was day,
Our Lord, our God, he called on us,
And bid us awake and pray.

Awake, awake, good people all,
Awake, and you shall hear,
Our Lord, our God, died on the Cross
For us whom He loved so dear.

O fair, O fair Jerusalem,
When shall I come to thee?
When shall my sorrows have an end,
Thy joy that I may see?

The fields were green as green could be,
When from His glorious seat
Our Lord, our God, He watered us,
With His dew so sweet.

And for the saving of our souls,
  Christ died upon the Cross;
We ne'er shall do for Jesus Christ
  As He has done for us.

The life of man is but a span,
  And cut down in its flower;
We are here to-day and to-morrow are gone
  We are all dead in an hour.

O pray teach your children, man,
  The while that you are here;
It will be better for your soul
  When your corpse lies on the bier.

To-day you may be alive, dear man,
  Worth many a thousand pound;
To-morrow may be dead, dear man,
  And your body laid under ground.

With one turf at your head, O man,
  And another at your feet,
Thy good deeds and thy bad, O man,
  Will all together meet.

My song is done, I must be gone,
  I can stay no longer here.
God bless you all, both great and small,
  And send you a Happy New Year!

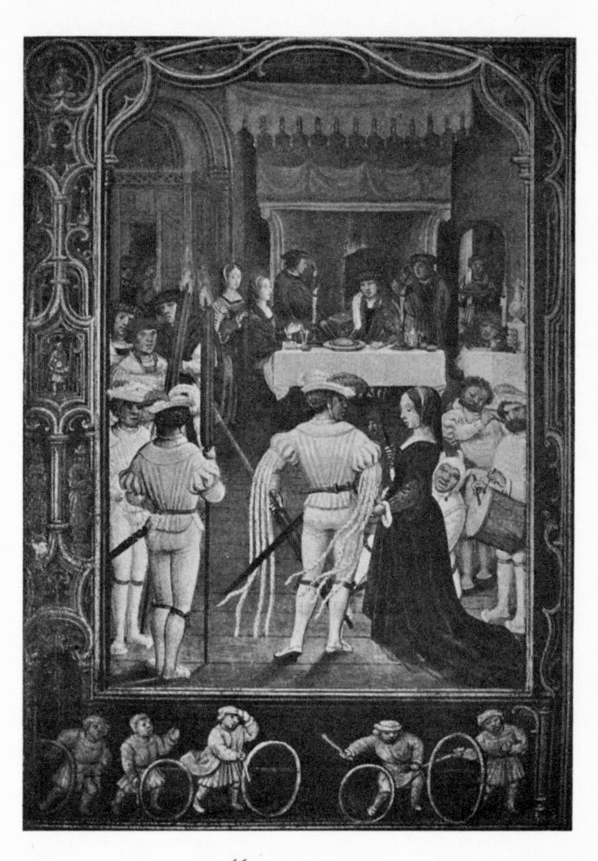

Make we merry

IN DULCI IUBILO[1]

Be Merry

Fifteenth Century.

Be merry, be merry, I pray you, be merry every one.

A PRINCIPAL point of charity,
It is merry to be
In Him that is but One.
Be merry, be merry, I pray you, be merry every one.

For He that is but One in bliss
To us hath sent His son, ywis,[2]
To save us from our fone.[3]
Be merry, be merry, I pray you, be merry every one.

For of a maiden a Child was born,
To save mankind that was forlorn.
Man, think thereon.
Be merry, be merry, I pray you, be merry every one.

[1] See note. [2] Verily. [3] Foes.

Now Mary, for thy Son His sake,
Save them all that mirth do make,
  And hold the longest on.
    Be merry, be merry, I pray you, be merry every one.

Now Make we Merry, All and Some

Fifteenth Century.

Now make we merry, all and some,
For Christmas now is come
  That hath no peer.
  Sing we all in fere.
    Now joy and bliss
    They shall not miss
  That make good cheer.

Now God Almighty down hath sent
The Holy Ghost to be present,
To light on Mary maiden verament,
That bare the Son of God with good intent,
  That hath no peer.
  Sing we all in fere.
    Now joy and bliss
    They shall not miss
  That make good cheer.

Now Godës Son omnipotent
In Mary mild He here hath ta'en
Flesh and blood, for He hath meant
Man to restore unto His gain,

That hath no peer.
Sing we all in fere.
Now joy and bliss
They shall not miss
That make good cheer.

To Mary mild our hearts be bent,
That blissful lady so be-kent,[1]
To pray that we be not undone,
Through Jesus Christ her gentle Son,
That hath no peer.
Sing we all in fere.
Now joy and bliss
They shall not miss
That make good cheer.

The Five Joys

Fifteenth Century.

I MAY sing of a may,
Of joys five and mirthës most.
The first joy, as I you tell,
With Mary met Saint Gabriel.
" Hail, Mary, I greet thee well
With Father, Son and Holy Ghost."

The second joy, in good fay,
Was on Christmas Day;
Born He was of a may
With Father, Son and Holy Ghost.

[1] Be-kent=well known ; *text:* be bent.

The third joy, withouten strife,
That blissful Birth was full rife,
When He rose fro death to life,
With Father, Son and Holy Ghost.

The fourth joy, in good fay,
Was upon Hallowed Thursday,
He rose to heaven in rich array,
With Father, Son and Holy Ghost.

The fifth joy, withouten dene,[1]
In heaven He crowned His mother clean,
That was well with the eye a-seen,[2]
With Father, Son and Holy Ghost.

In Dulci Iubilo

About 1567. John Wedderburn.

Now let us sing with mirth and joy,
Our heart's consolation
Lies *in præsepio,*
And shines as the sun,
Matris in gremio.
Alpha is and O, Alpha is and O.
O Jesu parvule,
I thirst sore after Thee,
Comfort my heart and mind,
O Puer optime!

God of all grace so kind,
Et Princeps Gloriæ,
Trahe me post Te,

[1] Doubt. [2] *Text:* wol wil the eyr a sene.

Trahe me post Te.
Ubi sunt gaudia;
In any place but there
Where that the angels sing,
Nova cantica,
But and the bells ring,
In Regis curia.
God if I were there,
God if I were there!

Now let us Sing with Joy and Mirth

About 1567. John Wedderburn.

Now let us sing with joy and mirth,
In honour of our Lordës birth,
For His lufe and humanity,
Who gave Himself for us to die.

By Adam we were all forlorn,
But now Christ Jesus till us is born,
Has freed us fra captivity,
And vanquished has our enemy.

When He was born nane did Him snib,
To lie richt law intill ane crib;
Ane ox, ane ass, richt tenderly
Refreshit His humanity.

His Godheid needeth na support
For it was full of all comfort,
Whilk equal is in all degree,
Unto His Father's majesty.

The angels sang with merryness,
Unto the herds, both mair and less,
And bade them of good comfort be,
For Christës new Nativity.

For ye were all at Godës horn,
This Babe, to you that now is born,
Sall make you safe, and for you die,
And you restore to liberty.

This Babe for you did shed His blude,
And tholit death upon the Rood;
And for His great humanity,
Exaltit is His Majesty.

And now He is our advocate,
Praying for us, baith ere and late;
This can the Scripture verify,
In sa far as ane man is He.

Therefore, all tide and time and hour,
Pass unto Him as Mediator
Betwix the Father's wrath and thee,
Of sin if thou would cleansëd be.

For He has promised with His heart
To all sinners that will revert
And fra their sinful life will flee,
Sall ring with Him eternally.

To God the Father must be gloir,
And also to Christ forever more;
The Holy Ghaist must blissit be,
Worker of this Nativity.

All the merrier is that place,
The sun of grace Him shineth[1] *in*

Fifteenth Century.

THE sun of grace Him shineth[1] in,
On a day when it was morrow,
When our Lord God born was,
Without sin or sorrow.
The sun of grace Him shineth in,
On a day when it was prime,
When our Lord God born was;
So well He knew His time.
The sun of grace Him shineth in,
On a day when it was noon,
When our Lord God born was,
And on the Rood [y]done.
The sun of grace Him shineth in,
On a day when it was undern,
When our Lord God born was,
And to the heart [y]stungen.[2]

Man, be joyful and mirth thou make,
For Christ is made man for thy sake

Temp. Henry VII. or VIII.

MAN, be merry, I thee rede,
But beware what mirths thou make;
Christ is clothëd in thy weed,
And He is made man for thy sake.

[1] *Text:* schynit. See note. [2] Pierced.

He came fro His Father's seat,
  Into this world to be thy make;[1]
Man, beware how thou Him treat,
  For He is made man for thy sake.

Look thou mercy ever cry,
  Now and alway, rathe and late;
And He will set thee wonder high,
  For He is made man for thy sake.

For Christmas Day

1574-1656. Bishop Hall.

IMMORTAL Babe, who this dear day
Did'st change Thine heaven for our clay,
And did'st with flesh Thy Godhead veil,
Eternal Son of God, all hail!

Shine, happy star; ye angels, sing
Glory on high to heaven's King;
Run, shepherds, leave your nightly watch,
See heaven come down to Bethlehem's cratch.

Worship, ye sages of the east,
The King of gods in meanness dressed;
O blessed maid, smile and adore
The God thy womb and arms have bore.

Star, angels, shepherds, and wise sages,
Thou virgin glory of all ages,
Restorëd frame of heaven and earth,
Joy in your dear Redeemer's birth!

[1] Comrade.

Cast off all Doubtful Care[1]

1589.

Cast off all doubtful care,
  Exile and banish tears;
To joyful news divine
  Lend us your listening ears.

An earthly tree a heavenly fruit it bare,
  A case of clay contained a crown immortal,
A crown of crowns, a King whose cost and care
  Redeemed poor man, whose race before was thrall
 To death, to doom, to pains of everlasting,
 By His sweet death, scores, stripes and often fasting.

A star above the stars, a sun of light,
  Whose blessed beams this wretched earth bespread
With hope of heaven and of God's Son the sight,
  Which in our flesh and sinful soul lay dead.
 O faith, O hope, O joys renowned forever,
 O lively death that deathless shall persever!

Then let us sing the lullabies of sleep
  To this sweet Babe, born to awake us all
From drowsy sin that made old Adam weep,
  And by his fault gave to mankind the fall.
 For lo! this day, the birthday, day of days,
 Summons our songs to give Him laud and praise.

[1] Byrd's *Songs of Sundry Natures.*

This Day Christ was Born[1]

1611.

THIS day Christ was born,
This day our Saviour did appear,
This day the angels sing in earth,
This day archangels are glad;
This day the just rejoice, saying:
Glory be to God on high,
Allelujah!

A Christmas Carol

1592–1644. Francis Quarles.[2]

GLORY to God on high, and jolly mirth
'Twixt man and man, and peace on earth!
This night a Child is born;
This night a Son is given;
This Son, this Child
Hath reconciled
Poor man that was forlorn,
And the angry God of heaven.
Hosanna, sing Hosanna!

Now, now that joyful day,
That blessed hour is come,
That was foretold
In days of old,
Wherein all nations may
Bless, bless the virgin's womb.
Hosanna, sing Hosanna!

[1] Byrd's *Psalms, Songs, and Sonnets.*
[2] *Eclogue* v (*The Shepherd's Oracles*).

Let heaven triumph above,
Let earth rejoice below;
Let heaven and earth
Be filled with mirth,
For peace and lasting love
Atones your God and you.
Hosanna, sing Hosanna!

There Comes a Ship

About 1550.

THERE comes a ship far sailing then,
Saint Michael was the steersman,
Saint John sat in the horn;
Our Lord harped, our Lady sang,
And all the bells of heaven they rang,
On Christ's Sunday at morn.

I Saw Three Ships[1]

Traditional.

I SAW three ships come sailing in
On Christmas day, on Christmas day;
I saw three ships come sailing in
On Christmas day in the morning.

And what was in those ships all three,
On Christmas day, on Christmas day?
And what was in those ships all three,
On Christmas day in the morning?

[1] See note.

Our Saviour Christ and His Lady,
On Christmas day, on Christmas day;
Our Saviour Christ and His Lady,
On Christmas day in the morning.

Pray whither sailed those ships all three,
On Christmas day, on Christmas day?
Pray whither sailed those ships all three,
On Christmas day in the morning?

O they sailed into Bethlehem,
On Christmas day, on Christmas day;
O they sailed into Bethlehem,
On Christmas day in the morning.

And all the bells on earth shall ring,
On Christmas day, on Christmas day;
And all the bells on earth shall ring,
On Christmas day in the morning.

And all the angels in Heaven shall sing,
On Christmas day, on Christmas day;
And all the angels in Heaven shall sing,
On Christmas day in the morning.

And all the souls on earth shall sing,
On Christmas day, on Christmas day;
And all the souls on earth shall sing,
On Christmas day in the morning.

Then let us all rejoice amain,
On Christmas day, on Christmas day;
Then let us all rejoice amain,
On Christmas day in the morning.

Christ's Nativity[1]

1650–65. Henry Vaughan.

Awake, glad heart! get up and sing!
It is the birthday of thy King.
Awake! Awake!
The sun doth shake
Light from his locks, and all the way
Breathing perfumes, doth spice the day.

Awake! awake! hark how th' wood rings,
Winds whisper, and the busy springs
A concert make.
Awake! Awake!
Man is their high priest, and should rise
To offer up the sacrifice.

I would I were some bird, or star,
Fluttering in woods, or lifted far
Above this inn
And road of sin;
Then either star or bird should be
Shining or singing still to Thee.

I would I had in my best part
Fit rooms for Thee! or that my heart
Were so clean as
Thy manger was!
But I am all filth, and obscene;
Yet, if Thou wilt, Thou can'st make me clean.

[1] *Silex Scintillans.*

Sweet Jesu ! will then. Let no more
This leper haunt and soil Thy door !
Cure him, ease him,
O release him !
And let once more, by mystic birth,
The Lord of life be born in earth.

PART III

CAROLS OF YULETIDE FESTIVITY

PROFACE

Proface

Temp. Henry VII. or VIII.

Proface,[1] welcome, welcome!
This time is born a Child of grace,
That for us mankind [2] hath take.
Proface.

A king's son and an emperour
Is come out of a maiden's tower,
With us to dwell with great honour.
Proface.

This holy time of Christëmas,
All sorrow and sin we should release,
And cast away all heaviness.
Proface.

The good lord of this place entire,
Saith welcome to all that now appear,
Unto such fare as ye find here.
Proface.

[1] Much good may it do you!

[2] Man's nature.

Welcome be this new year!
And look ye all be of good cheer.
Our Lord God be us ever near! [1]
Proface.

In Die Nativitatis

Temp. Henry VII. or VIII.

"*Nowell, nowell, nowell, nowell.*"
"Who is there that singeth so *nowell, nowell, nowell?*"

"I am here, Sir Christëmas."
"Welcome, my lord Sir Christëmas,
Welcome to us all, both more and less,
Come near, nowell."

"*Dieus wous garde, bewe sieurs,*[2] tidings I you bring:
A maid hath borne a child full ying,
The which causeth [you] for to sing,
Nowell.

"Christ is now born of a pure maid,
In an ox-stall he is laid,
Wherefore sing we alle at a brayde,[3]
Nowell.

"*Bevvex bien par tutte la company,*
Make good cheer and be right merry,
And sing with us now joyfully,
Nowell."

[1] *Text:* at our dewre=need.
[2] *Elsewhere* byewe syre.
[3] In unison.

Good Day, Good Day

Fifteenth Century.

Good day, good day,
My Lord Sir Christëmas, good day!

Good day, Sir Christëmas our King,
For every man, both old and ying,
Is glad of your coming.
Good day.

Godës Son so much of might
From heaven to earth down is light
And born is of a maid so bright.
Good day.

Heaven and earth and also hell
And all that ever in them dwell,
Of your coming they be full snell.
Good day.

All manner of mirthës we will make,
And solace to our heartës take,
My seemly lordë for your sake.
Good day.

What cheer? Good cheer! Good cheer! Good cheer! Be merry and glad this good New Year.

Before 1536.

Lift up your heartës and be glad!
In Christës birth the angel bade;
Say each to other, if any be sad:
What cheer? Good cheer! Good cheer! Good cheer!
Be merry and glad this good New Year.

Now the King of heaven His birth hath take,
Joy and mirth we ought to make!
Say each to other, for his sake:
What cheer? Good cheer! Good cheer! Good cheer!
Be merry and glad this good New Year.

I tell you all with heart so free,
Right welcome ye be [all] to me.
Be glad and merry for charity!
What cheer? Good cheer! Good cheer! Good cheer!
Be merry and glad this good New Year.

The goodman of this place in fere[1]
You to be merry he prayeth you here;
And with good heart he doth to you say:
What cheer? Good cheer! Good cheer! Good cheer!
Be merry and glad this good New Year.

Make we merry, both more and less,
For now is the time of Christëmas

Before 1536.

Let no man come into this hall,
Groom, page nor yet marshall,
But that some sport he bring withal,
For now is the time of Christëmas.

If that he say he cannot sing,
Some other sport then let him bring,
That it may please at this feasting,
For now is the time of Christëmas.

[1] Company.

If he say he can naught do,
Then for my love ask him no mo,
But to the stocks then let him go,
For now is the time of Christëmas.

Now Christmas Draweth Near

1558–1626. Nicholas Breton.

Now Christmas draweth near, and most men make good cheer,
With heigh-ho, care away!
I, like a sickly mome, in drowsy dumps at home,
Will naught but fast and pray.

Some sing and dance for life, some card and dice as rife,
Some use old Christmas games;
But I, oh wretched wight! in dole both day and night,
Must dwell; the world so frames.

In Court, what pretty toys, what fine and pleasant joys,
To pass the time away!
In country naught but care; sour cheese-curds, chiefest fare;
For wine, a bowl of whey.

For every dainty dish, of flesh or else of fish,
And for your drink in Court,
A dish of young fried frogs, sod houghs of meazled hogs,
A cup of small tap wort.

And for each courtly sight, each show that may delight
The eye or else the mind;
In country thorns and brakes, and many miry lakes,
Is all the good you find.

And for fine enteries, halls, chambers, galleries,
And lodgings many mo;
Here dessert woods and plains, where no delight remains,
To walk in to and fro.

In Court, for to be short, for every pretty sport
That may the heart delight;
In country many a grief, and small or no relief,
To aid the wounded wight.

And in this desert place, I, wretch! in woeful case,
This merry Christmas time,
Content myself perforce to rest my careful corse,
And so I end my rhyme.

The Christmas Now is Past

1558–1626. Nicholas Breton.

The Christmas now is past, and I have kept my fast,
With prayer every day;
And, like a country clown, with nodding up and down,
Have passed the time away.

As for old Christmas games, or dancing with fine dames,
Or shows, or pretty plays;
A solemn oath I swear, I came not where they were,
Not all these holy days.

I did not sing one note, except it were by rote,
Still buzzing like a bee;
To ease my heavy heart of some though little smart,
For want of other glee.

And as for pleasant wine, there was no drink so fine,
For to be tasted here;
Full simple was my fare, if that I should compare,
The same to Christmas cheer.

I saw no kind of sight that might my mind delight,
Believe me, noble dame;
But everything I saw did fret at woe my maw,
To think upon the same.

Upon some bushy balk full fain I was to walk,
In woods, from tree to tree,
For want of better room; but since my fatal doom
Hath so appointed me;

I stood therewith content, the Christmas full was spent,
In hope that God will send
A better yet next year, my heavy heart to cheer;
And so I make an end.

Make we mirth for Christës birth,
And sing we Yule till Candlemas

Fifteenth Century.

The first day of Yule have we in mind,
How God was man born of our kind,
For He the bonds would unbind
Of all our sins and wickedness.

The second day we sing of Stephen
That stonëd [was] and stied [1] up even
To God that he saw stand in heaven,
And crownëd was for his prowess.

[1] Ascended.

The third day 'longeth to St. John,
That was Christ's darling, dearer none,
To whom He betook,[1] when He should gone,
His mother dear for his cleanness.

The fourth day, of the children young,
That Herod to death had done with wrong;
Of Christ they could not tell with tongue,
But with their blood bare Him witness.

The fifth day 'longeth to St. Thomas,[2]
That as a strong pillar of brass
Held up the Church and slain he was,
For he stood [fast] in righteousness.

The eighth day took Jesu His name,
That saved mankind fro sin and shame,
And circumcised was for no blame,
But for ensample of meekness.

The twelfth day offered to Him kings three,
Gold, myrrh, incense, these giftës free,
For God and man and king is He;
Thus worshipped they His worthiness.

The fourteenth day came Mary mild,
Into the Temple with her Child,
To show her clean that was never defiled,
And therewith endeth Christmas.

[1] Entrusted. [2] Thomas à Becket.

Christmas

1558. Thomas Tusser.

GET ivy and hull,[1] woman, deck up thine house,
And take this same brawn for to seethe and to souse;
Provide us good cheer, for thou knowest the old guise,
Old customs that good be, let no man despise.
At Christmas be merry and thank God of all,
And feast thy poor neighbours, the great and the small.
Yea, all the year long have an eye to the poor,
And God shall send luck to keep open thy door.
Good fruit and good plenty do well in thy loft,
Then lay for an orchard and cherish it oft.
The profit is mickle, the pleasure is much;
At pleasure with profit few wise men will grutch.
For plants and for stocks lay aforehand to cast,
But set or remove them, while Twelve-tide [2] do last.

Now have good day, now have good day!
I am Christmas, and now I go my way

Before 1536.

HERE have I dwelled with more and less
From Hallowtide till Candlemas,
And now must I from you hence pass;
Now have good day!

I take my leave of king and knight,
And earl, baron and lady bright,
To wilderness I must me dight;
Now have good day!

[1] Holly. [2] Christmas to Twelfth Night.

And at the good lord of this hall
I take my leave, and of guestës all.
Methinks I hear, Lent doth call;
Now have good day!

And at every worthy officer,
Marshall, panter and butler,
I take my leave as for this year;
Now have good day!

Another year I trust I shall
Make merry in this hall,
If rest and peace in England may fall;
Now have good day!

But oftentimes I have heard say
That he is loth to part away,
That often biddeth "have good day";
Now have good day!

Now fare ye well, all in fere!
Now fare ye well for all this year!
Yet for my sake, have good cheer;
Now have good day!

A Christmas Carol[1]

1622. George Wither.

So, now is come our joyfullest feast;
Let every man be jolly.
Each room with ivy leaves is dressed,
And every post with holly.

[1] *Juvenilia.*

Though some churls at our mirth repine,
Round your foreheads garlands twine;
Drown sorrow in a cup of wine,
  And let us all be merry.

Now all our neighbours' chimneys smoke,
  And Christmas blocks are burning;
Their ovens they with baked meats choke,
  And all their spits are turning.
Without the door let sorrow lie;
And if for cold it hap to die,
We'll bury't in a Christmas pie,
  And evermore be merry.

Now every lad is wondrous trim,
  And no man minds his labour;
Our lasses have provided them
  A bag-pipe and a tabor;
Young men and maids, and girls and boys,
Give life to one another's joys;
And you anon shall by their noise
  Perceive that they are merry.

Rank misers now do sparing shun;
  Their hall of music soundeth;
And dogs thence with whole shoulders run,
  So all things there aboundeth.
The country folks themselves advance
With crowdy muttons out of France;
And Jack shall pipe and Jill shall dance,
  And all the town be merry.

Ned Squash hath fetched his bands from pawn,
  And all his best apparel;
Brisk Nell hath bought a ruff of lawn
  With dropping of the barrel;
And those that hardly all the year
Had bread to eat, or rags to wear,
Will have both clothes and dainty fare,
  And all the day be merry.

Now poor men to the justices
  With capons make their errands;
And if they hap to fail of these,
  They plague them with their warrants;
But now they feed them with good cheer,
And what they want they take in beer;
For Christmas comes but once a year,
  And then they shall be merry.

Good farmers in the country nurse
  The poor, that else were undone;
Some landlords spend their money worse
  On lust and pride at London.
There the roysters they do play,
Drab and dice their lands away,
Which may be ours another day;
  And therefore let's be merry.

The client now his suit forbears,
  The prisoner's heart is eased;
The debtor drinks away his cares,
  And for the time is pleased.

Though other purses be more fat,
Why should we pine or grieve at that?
Hang sorrow! care will kill a cat,
  And therefore let's be merry.

Hark! how the wags abroad do call
  Each other forth to rambling;
Anon you'll see them in the hall
  For nuts and apples scrambling.
Hark! how the roofs with laughter sound!
Anon they'll think the house goes round,
For they the cellar's depth have found,
  And there they will be merry.

The wenches with their wassel-bowls
  About the streets are singing;
The boys are come to catch the owls,
  The wild mare is in bringing.
Our kitchen boy hath broke his box,
And to the dealing of the ox
Our honest neighbours come by flocks,
  And here they will be merry.

Now kings and queens poor sheep cots have,
  And mate with everybody;
The honest now may have the knave,
  And wise men play the noddy.
Some youths will now a-mumming go,
Some others play at Rowland-ho,
And twenty other gameboys mo,
  Because they will be merry.

Then wherefore in these merry days
  Should we, I pray, be duller?
No, let us sing some roundelays,
  To make our mirth the fuller.
And whilst thus inspired we sing,
Let all the streets with echoes ring,
Woods and hills and everything,
  Bear witness we are merry.

A Christmas Carol

1648. Robert Herrick.

Chorus. WHAT sweeter music can we bring,
Than a carol, for to sing
The birth of this our heavenly King?
Awake the voice! Awake the string!
Heark, ear, and eye, and everything,
Awake! the while the active finger
Runs divisions with the singer.

(*From the flourish they come to the song.*)

Dark and dull night, fly hence away,
And give the honour to this day,
That sees December turn'd to May.
If we may ask the reason, say
The why and wherefore all things here
Seem like the springtime of the year?
Why does the chilling winter's morn
Smile like a field beset with corn?
Or smell like to a mead new-shorn,

Thus on the sudden? Come and see
The cause why things thus fragrant be:
'Tis He is born whose quickening birth
Gives life and lustre public mirth
To heaven and the under-earth.

Chorus. We see Him come, and know Him ours,
Who with His sunshine and His showers
Turns all the patient ground to flowers.

The Darling of the world is come,
And fit it is we find a room
To welcome Him. The nobler part
Of all the house here, is the heart.

Chorus. Which we will give him; and bequeath
This holly and this ivy wreath,
To do him honour who's our King,
The Lord of all this revelling.

The New Year is Begun[1]

Seventeenth Century.

THE New Year is begun,
Good morrow, my masters all!
The cheerful rising sun
Now shining in this hall,
Brings mirth and joy
To man and boy
With all that here do dwell;
Whom Jesus bless
With love's increase,
So all things shall prosper well.

[1] *New Christmas Carols.* (Oxford. Undated.)

A New Year's gift I bring
Unto my master here,
Which is a welcome thing
Of mirth and merry cheer.
A New Year's lamb
Come from thy dam
An hour before daybreak;
Your noted ewe
Doth this bestow,
Good master, for your sake.

And to my dame so kind
This New Year's gift I bring;
I'll bear an honest mind
Unto her whilst I live.
Your white-wooled sheep
I'll safely keep
From harm of bush or briar,
That garments gay
For your array
May clothe you the next New Year.

And to your children all,
These New Year's gifts I bring;
And though the price be small,
They're fit for queen or king:
Fair pippins red
Kept in my bed
A-mellowing since last year,
Whose beauty bright
So clear of sight
Their hearts will glad and cheer.

And to your maids and men
I bring both points and pins;
Come bid me welcome then,
The good New Year begins;
And for my love
Let me approve
The friendship of your maid,
Whose nappy ale
So good and stale
Will make my wits afraid.

I dare not with it deal
But in a sober diet.
If I, poor shepherd, steal
A draught to be unquiet,
And lose my way
This New Year's day
As I go to my fold,
You'll surely think
My love of drink
This following year will hold.

Here stands my bottle and hook,
Good kitchen-maid, draw near;
Thou art an honest cook,
And canst brew ale and beer;
Thy office show
Before I go,
My bottle and bag come fill;
And for thy sake
I'll merry make
Upon the next green hill.

All You that are Good Fellows[1]

1642.

All you that are good fellows,
  Come hearken to my song;
I know you do not hate good cheer
  Nor liquor that is strong.
I hope there is none here
  But soon will take my part,
Seeing my master and my dame
  Says welcome with their heart.

This is a time of joyfulness
  And merry time of year,
Whereas the rich with plenty stored
  Doth make the poor good cheer;
Plum-porridge, roast-beef, and minced pies
  Stand smoking on the board,
With other brave varieties
  Our master doth afford.

Our mistress and her cleanly maids
  Have neatly played the cooks;
Methinks these dishes eagerly
  At my sharp stomach looks,
As though they were afraid
  To see me draw my blade;
But I revenged on them will be
  Until my stomach's stayed.

[1] *New Christmas Carols.*

Come fill us of the strongest,
  Small drink is out of date;
Methinks I shall fare like a prince
  And sit in gallant state.
This is no miser's feast,
  Although that things be dear;
God grant the founder of this feast
  Each Christmas keep good cheer.

This day for Christ we celebrate
  Who was born at this time;
For which all Christians should rejoice
  And I do sing in rhyme.
When you have given God thanks,
  Unto your dainties fall.
Heaven bless my master and my dame,
  Lord bless me and you all!

Come, Mad Boys[1]

1642.

COME, mad boys, be glad, boys, for Christmas is here,
And we shall be feasted with jolly good cheer;
  Then let us be merry, 'tis Saint Stephen's day,
  Let's eat and drink freely, here's nothing to pay.

My master bids you welcome, and so doth my dame,
And 'tis yonder smoking dish doth me inflame;
  Anon I'll be with you, though you me outface,
  For now I do tell you I have time and place.

[1] *New Christmas Carols.*

I'll troll the bowl to you, then let it go round,
My heels are so light they can stand on no ground;
  My tongue it doth chatter, and goes pitter patter,
  Here's good beer and strong beer, for I will not flatter.

And now for remembrance of blessed Saint Stephen,
Let's joy at morning, at noon, and at even;
  Then leave off your mincing, and fall to mince pies,
  I pray take my counsel, be ruled by the wise.

With Merry Glee and Solace[1]

1661.

WITH merry glee and solace
This second day of Christmas
  Now comes in bravely to my master's house,
    Where plenty of good cheer I see,
    With that which most contenteth me,
  As brawn and bacon, powdered beef and sauce.

For the love of Stephen,
That blessed saint of heaven,
  Which stonëd was for Jesus Christ his sake,
    Let us all both more and less
    Cast away all heaviness,
  And in a sober manner merry make.

He was a man beloved,
And his faith approved
  By suffering death [up]on this holy day,
    Where he with gentle patience,
    And a constant sufferance,
  Hath taught us all to heaven the ready way.

[1] *New Carolls for the Mery Time of Christmas.*

So let our mirth be civil,
That not one thought of evil
May take possession of our hearts at all,
So shall we love and favour get
Of them that kindly thus do set
Their bounties here so freely in this hall.

Of delicates so dainty,
I see here is plenty
Upon this table ready here prepared;
Then let us now give thanks to those
That all things friendly thus bestows,
Esteeming not this world that is so hard.

For of the same my master
Hath made me here a taster;
The Lord above requite him for the same!
And so to all within this house
I will drink a full carouse,
With leave of my good master and my dame.

And, the Lord be praised,
My stomach is well eased,
My bones at quiet may go take their rest;
Good fortune surely followed me
To bring me thus so luckily
To eat and drink so freely of the best.

All You that in this House be Here[1]

1661.

All you that in this house be here,
  Remember Christ that for us died,
And spend away with modest cheer,
  In loving sort, this Christmastide.

And whereas plenty God hath sent,
  Give frankly to your friends in love;
The bounteous mind is freely bent,
  And never will a niggard prove.

Our table spread within the hall,
  I know a banquet is at hand,
And friendly sort to welcome all
  That will unto their tacklings stand.

The maids are bonny girls I see,
  Who have provided much good cheer,
Which at my dame's commandment be
  To set it on the table here.

For I have here two knives in store
  To lend to him that wanteth one;
Commend my wits, good lads, therefore,
  That comes now here having none.

For if I should, no Christmas pie
  Would fall, I doubt, unto my share;
Wherefore I will my manhood try,
  To fight a battle if I dare.

[1] *New Carolls for the Mery Time of Christmas.*

For pastry crust, like castle walls,
  Stands braving me unto my face;
I am not well until it falls
  And I made captain of the place.

The prunes so lovely look on me,
  I cannot choose but venture on;
The pie-meat spicëd brave I see,
  The which I must not let alone.

Then, butler, fill me forth some beer,
  My song hath made me somewhat dry;
And so again to this good cheer,
  I'll quickly fall courageously.

And for my master I will pray,
  With all that of his household are,
Both old and young, that long we may
  Of God's good blessing have a share.

Come Follow, Follow Me[1]

1688.

Come follow, follow me,
Those that good fellows be,
    Into the buttery
    Our manhood for to try;
The master keeps a bounteous house,
And gives leave freely to carouse.

[1] *New Christmas Carols.*

Then wherefore should we fear,
Seeing here is store of cheer?
    It shows but cowardice
    At this time to be nice.
Then boldly draw your blades and fight,
For we shall have a merry night.

When we have done this fray,
Then we will go to play
    At cards or else at dice,
    And be rich in a trice;
Then let the knaves go round apace,
I hope each time to have an ace.

Come, maids, let's waste no beer
After our Christmas cheer,
    And I will duly crave
    Good husbands you may have,
And that you may good houses keep,
Where we may drink carouses deep.

And when that['s] spent the day,
We'll Christmas gambols play,
    At hot cockles beside,
    And then go to all-hide,
With many other pretty toys,
Men, women, youths, maids, girls and boys.

Come, let's dance round the hall,
And let's for liquor call;
    Put apples in the fire,
    Sweet maids, I you desire;
And let a bowl be spiced well,
Of happy stuff that doth excel.

Twelve days we now have spent
In mirth and merriment,
    And daintily did fare,
    For which we took no care;
But now I sadly call to mind
What days of sorrow are behind.

We must leave off to play,
To-morrow's working day;
    According to each calling
    Each man must now be falling,
And ply his business all the year,
Next Christmas for to make good cheer.

Now of my master kind,
Good welcome I did find,
    And of my loving mistress,
    This merry time of Christmas;
For which to them great thanks I give,
God grant they long together live.

Now Thrice Welcome, Christmas[1]

1695.

Now thrice welcome, Christmas,
    Which brings us good cheer,
Minc'd pies and plum porridge,
    Good ale and strong beer;
With pig, goose and capon,
    The best that can be,
So well doth the weather
    And our stomachs agree.

[1] *Poor Robin's Almanac.*

Observe how the chimneys
  Do smoke all about,
The cooks are providing
  For dinner, no doubt;
But those on whose tables
  No victuals appear,
O may they keep Lent
  All the rest of the year!

With holly and ivy
  So green and so gay,
We deck up our houses
  As fresh as the day,
With bays and rosemary,
  And laurel complete;
And every one now
  Is a king in conceit.

WASSAIL[1]

Wassail

About 1548. John Bale.[2]

WASSAIL, wassail, out of the milk pail,
Wassail, wassail, as white as my nail,
Wassail, wassail, in snow, frost and hail,
Wassail, wassail, with partridge and rail,
Wassail, wassail, that much doth avail,
Wassail, wassail, that never will fail.

Wassail, wassail, wassail, sing we,
In worship of Christ's Nativity

Before 1536.

Now joy be to the Trinity,
  Father, Son and Holy Ghost,
That One God is in Trinity,
  Father of heaven, of mightës most.
    Wassail, wassail, wassail, sing we,
    In worship of Christ's nativity!

And joy be to the virgin pure,
  That ever kept her undefiled,
Grounded in grace, in heart full sure,
  And bare a child as maiden mild.
    Wassail, wassail, wassail, sing we,
    In worship of Christ's nativity!

[1] See note. [2] *King John.*

Bethlehem and the star so sheen,
That shone three kingës for to guide,
Bear witness of this maiden clean;
The kingës three offered that tide.
Wassail, wassail, wassail, sing we,
In worship of Christ's nativity!

And shepherds heard, as written is,
The joyful song that there was sung,
"*Gloria in excelsis!*"
With angel's voice it was out-rung.
Wassail, wassail, wassail, sing we,
In worship of Christ's nativity!

Now joy be to the blessedful Child
And joy be to His mother dear;
Joy we all of that maiden mild,
And joy have they that make good cheer!
Wassail, wassail, wassail, sing we,
In worship of Christ's nativity!

Omnes Gentes Plaudite

Fifteenth Century.

Omnes gentes plaudite,
I saw many birds sitting on a tree;
They took their flight and flew away,
With, *Ego dixi*, have good day!
Many white feathers hath the pie—
I may no more sing, my lips are so dry.
Many white feathers hath the swan—
The more that I drink, the less good I can.
Lay sticks on the fire, well may it burn; [1]
Give us once to drink ere away we turn.[2]

[1] *Text:* wyl mot is brenne. [2] *Text:* ere we gon henne.

Bring us in Good Ale[1]

Temp. Henry VI.

Bring us in good ale, and bring us in good ale;
For our Blessed Lady's sake, bring us in good ale.

Bring us in no brown bread, for that is made of bran,
Nor bring us in no white bread, for therein is no game;
But bring us in good ale.

Bring us in no beef, for there is many bones,
But bring us in good ale, for that goes down at once;
And bring us in good ale.

Bring us in no bacon, for that is passing fat,
But bring us in good ale, and give us enough of that;
And bring us in good ale.

Bring us in no mutton, for that is often lean,
Nor bring us in no tripes, for they be seldom clean;
But bring us in good ale.

Bring us in no eggs, for there are many shells,
But bring us in good ale, and give us nothing else;
And bring us in good ale.

Bring us in no butter, for therein are many hairs;
Nor bring us in no pig's flesh, for that will make us boars;
But bring us in good ale.

Bring us in no puddings, for therein is all God's good;
Nor bring us in no venison, for that is not for our blood;
But bring us in good ale.

Bring us in no capon's flesh, for that is often dear;
Nor bring us in no duck's flesh, for they slobber in the mere;
But bring us in good ale.

[1] See note.

A Bone, God Wot

Temp. Henry VIII.

A BONE, God wot,
Sticks in my throat;
Without I have a draught
    Of corny ale,
    Nappy and stale,
My life is in great waste.

    Some ale or beer,
    Gentle butler,
Some liquor thou us shew,
    Such as you mash,
    Our throats to wash,
The best ware that you brew.

Saint, master and knight,
That Saint Malt hight,
Were pressed between two stones,—
    That sweet humour
    Of his liquor
Would make us sing at once.

    Mr. Wortley,
    I dare well say,
I tell you as I think,
    Would not, I say,
    Bid us this day,
But that we should have drink.

His men so tall
Walks up his hall,
With many a comely dish;
    Of his good meat
    I cannot eat,
Without a drink ywis.

    Now give us drink.
    And let cat wink,
I tell you all at once,
    It sticks so sore,
    I may sing no more,
Till I have drunken once.

Come Bravely on, my Masters[1]

1642.

Come bravely on, my masters,
For here we shall be tasters
  Of curious dishes that are brave and fine;
    Where they that do such cheer afford,
    I'll lay my knife upon the board,
  My master and my dame they do not pine.

Who is't will not be merry
And sing down, down-a-derry?
  For now it is a time of joy and mirth;
    'Tis said 'tis merry in the hall
    Whenas beards they do wag all;
  God's plenty's here, it doth not show a dearth.

[1] *New Christmas Carols.*

Let him take all lives longest,
Come fill us of the strongest,
And I will drink a health to honest John;
Come pray thee, butler, fill the bowl,
And let it round the table troll,
When that is up I'll tell you more anon.

My Master and Dame, I well Perceive[1]

Seventeenth Century.

My master and dame, I well perceive,
Are purposed to be merry to-night,
And willingly hath given me leave
To combat with a Christmas knight.
Sir Pig, I see, comes prancing in
And bids me draw if that I dare;
I care not for his valour a pin,
For Jack of him will have a share.

My Lady Goose among the rest
Upon the table takes her place,
And piping-hot bids do my best,
And bravely looks me in the face;
For pigs and geese are gallant cheer,
God bless my master and dame therefore!
I trust before the next New Year
To eat my part of half a score.

I likewise see good minced-pie
Here standing swaggering on the table;
The lofty walls so large and high
I'll level down if I be able;

[1] *New Christmas Carols.* (Oxford. Undated.)

For they be furnished with good plums,
  And spicëd well with pepper and salt,
Every prune as big as both my thumbs
  To drive down bravely the juice of malt.

Fill me some of your Christmas beer,
  Your pepper sets my mouth on heat,
And Jack's a-dry with your good cheer,
  Give me some good ale to my meat.
And then again my stomach I'll show,
  For good roast-beef here stoutly stands;
I'll make it stoop before I go,
  Or I'll be no man of my hands.

And for the plenty of this house
  God keep it thus well-stored alway;
Come, butler, fill me a good carouse,
  And so we'll end our Christmas day.

A Jolly Wassail-Bowl[1]

Seventeenth Century.

A JOLLY wassail-bowl,
  A wassail of good ale,
Well fare the butler's soul,
  That setteth this to sale,
    Our jolly wassail.

Good dame, here at your door,
  Our wassail we begin;
We are all maidens poor,
  We pray now let us in
    With our wassail.

[1] *New Christmas Carols.* (Oxford. Undated.)

Our wassail we do fill
  With apples and with spice,
Then grant us your good will
  To taste here once or twice
    Of our wassail.

If any maidens be
  Here dwelling in this house,
They kindly will agree
  To take a full carouse
    Of our wassail.

But here they let us stand
  All freezing in the cold;
Good master, your command
  To enter and be bold
    With our wassail.

Much joy unto this hall
  With us is entered in;
Our master, first of all,
  We hope will now begin
    Of our wassail.

And after his good wife
  Our spicëd bowl will try;
The Lord prolong your life!
  Good fortune we espy
    For our wassail.

Some bounty from your hands,
  Our wassail to maintain,
We'll buy no home nor lands
  With that which we do gain
    With our wassail.

This is our merry night
  Of choosing king and queen;
Then, be it your delight,
  That something may be seen
    In our wassail.

It is a noble part
  To bear a liberal mind.
God bless our master's heart!
  For here we comfort find
    With our wassail.

And now we must be gone,
  To seek out more good cheer;
Where bounty will be shown
  As we have found it here
    With our wassail.

Much joy betide them all,
  Our prayers shall be still;
We hope and ever shall
  For this your great good will
    To our wassail.

Wassail, Wassail, all over the Town

Traditional.

WASSAIL, wassail, all over the town,
Our bread it is white, and our ale it is brown;
Our bowl it is made of the maplin tree,
So here, my good fellow, I'll drink it to thee.

The wassailing bowl, with a toast within,
Come, fill it up unto the brim;
Come, fill it up, that we may see;
With the wassailing bowl I'll drink to thee.

Come, butler, come bring us a bowl of your best;
And we hope your souls in heaven shall rest;
But if you do bring us a bowl of your small,
Then down shall go butler, the bowl and all.

O butler, O butler, now don't you be worst,
But pull out your knife and cut us a toast;
And cut us a toast, one that we may all see;
With the wassailing bowl I'll drink to thee.

Here's to Dobbin and to his right eye!
God send our mistress a good Christmas pie!
A good Christmas pie as e'er we did see;
With the wassailing bowl I'll drink to thee.

Here's to Broad May and to her [1] broad horn,
God send our master a good crop of corn,
A good crop of corn as we all may see;
With the wassailing bowl I'll drink to thee.

Here's to Colly and to her long tail,
We hope our master and mistress heart will ne'er fail;
But bring us a bowl of your good strong beer,
And then we shall taste of your Happy New Year.

[1] *Text:* his.

Be there here any pretty maids ? We hope there be some.
Don't let the jolly wassailers stand on the cold stone,
But open the door and pull out the pin,
That we jolly wassailers may all sail in.

The Wassailers' Carol

Traditional.

HERE we come a-wassailing
Among the leaves so green,
Here we come a-wandering
So fair to be seen.

Chorus. Love and joy come to you,
And to your wassail too,
And God send you a Happy New Year,
a New Year ;
And God send you a Happy New Year.
Our wassail cup is made of the rosemary tree,
So is your beer of the best barley.

We are not the daily beggars,
That beg from door to door,
But we are neighbours' children,
Whom you have seen before.

Call up the butler of this house,
Put on his golden ring,
Bid him bring up a glass of beer,
The better that we may sing.

We have got a little purse
Made of stretching leather skin ;
We want a little of your money
To line it well within.

Bring us out a table,
  And spread it with a cloth,
Bring us out a mouldy cheese,
  And some of your Christmas loaf.

God bless the master of this house,
  Likewise the mistress too;
And all the little children,
  That round the table go.

Good master and mistress,
  While you're sitting by the fire,
Pray think of us poor children,
  Who are wandering in the mire.

Here we Come A-Whistling

Traditional.

HERE we come a-whistling [1] through the fields so green;
Here we come a-singing, so fair to be seen.
  God send you happy, God send you happy,
  Pray God send you a Happy New Year!

The roads are very dirty, my boots are very thin,
I have a little pocket to put a penny in.
  God send you happy, God send you happy,
  Pray God send you a Happy New Year!

Bring out your little table and spread it with a cloth,
Bring out some of your old ale, likewise your Christmas loaf.
  God send you happy, God send you happy,
  Pray God send you a Happy New Year!

[1] *For* wassailing. Cf. preceding carol.

God bless the master of this house, likewise the mistress too;
And all the little children that round the table strew.
God send you happy, God send you happy,
Pray God send you a happy New Year!

As I Sat under a Sycamore Tree

Traditional.

As I sat under a sycamore tree, a sycamore tree, a sycamore tree,
I looked me out upon the sea,
A Christmas day in the morning.

I saw three ships a-sailing there, a-sailing there, a-sailing there,
The Virgin Mary and Christ they bare,[1]
A Christmas day in the morning.

He did whistle, and she did sing, she did sing, she did sing,
And all the bells on earth did ring,
A Christmas day in the morning.

And now we hope to taste your cheer, taste your cheer, taste your cheer,
And wish you all a Happy New Year,
A Christmas day in the morning.

[1] See note.

CAPUT APRI DEFERO[1]

Tidings I Bring You for to Tell

Fifteenth Century.

Tidings I bring you for to tell,
What me in wild forest befell,
When me must with a wild beast mell,[2]
With the boar so brim.[3]

A boar so brim that me pursued,
Me for to kill so sharply slued,[4]
That brimly [3] beast so cruel and rude,[5]
There tamed I him,
And reft fro him both life and limb.

Truly to show you that is true,
His head with my sword I hew,
To make this day mirth new to you,
Now eat thereof anon.

Eat and much good do it you,
Take your bread and mustard thereto,
Joy with me that I have thus done,
I pray you to be glad every one,
And joy all in one.

[1] See note. [2] Meddle. [3] Fierce.
[4] *Text:* ameved. [5] *Text:* unryde.

Po, po, po, po,
[I] love brawn and so do mo

Fifteenth Century.

At the beginning of the meat,
Of a boar's head ye shall eat,
And in the mustard ye shall wet;
And ye shall singen ere ye gone.[1]

Welcome be ye that be here,
And ye shall have right good cheer,
And also a right good fare;
And ye shall singen ere ye gone.

Welcome be ye every one,
For ye shall singen sithe [2] anon;
Hie you fast that ye had done,
And ye shall singen ere ye gone.

Hey, hey, hey, hey,
The boar's head is armëd Gay

Fifteenth Century.

The boar's head in hand I bring,
With garland gay in portering.
I pray you all with me to sing,
With hey.

Lords, knights, and squires,
Parsons, priests, and vicars,
The boar's head is the first mess,
With hey.

[1] Go. [2] After.

The boar's head, as I you say,
He takes his leave, and goeth his way,
Gone after the Twelfth till fit day,
With hey.

Then comes in the second course [1] with mickle pride,
The cranes, the herons, the bitterns by their side,
The partridges and the plovers, the woodcocks and the snipe,
With hey.

Larks in hot sauce, ladies for to pick,
Good drink thereto, luscious and fine,
Blwet of Allmayne,[2] Romney and wine,
With hey.

Good bread, ale and wine, dare I well say,
The boar's head with mustard armëd so gay;
Frumenty to pottage, with venison fine,
And the humbles of the doe, and all that ever comes in;
Capons ybaked with the pieces of the roe,
Raisins and currants,[3] with other spices mo.

In Die Nativitatis

Temp. Henry VII. or VIII.

Nowell, nowell, nowell, nowell,
Tidings good I think to tell.

The boar's head that we bring here,
Betokeneth a Prince withouten peer,
Is born this day to buy us dear,
Nowell.

[1] See note. [2] *For* bruet of Allmayne, *i.e.* German stew.
[3] *Literally*, raisins of currants, *the common expression of the time, meaning originally*, raisins of Corinth.

A boar is a sovereign beast,
And acceptable in every feast;
So might thy Lord be to most and least,
Nowell.

The boar's head we bring with song,
In worship of Him that thus sprung
Of a virgin to redress all wrong,
Nowell.

The Boar's Head in Hand bear I[1]

Traditional.

The boar's head in hand bear I,
Bedeck'd with bay and rosemary;
And I pray you, my masters, be merry,
Quot estis in convivio.
Caput apri defero,
Reddens laudes Domino.

The boar's head, as I understand,
Is the rarest dish in all this land,
Which thus bedeck'd with a gay garland,
Let us *servire cantico.*
Caput apri defero,
Reddens laudes Domino.

Our steward hath provided this,
In honour of the King of bliss;
Which on this day to be servëd is,
In reginensi atrio.
Caput apri defero,
Reddens laudes Domino.

[1] As sung at Queen's College, Oxford.

A Carol Bringing in the Boar's Head[1]

1521.

Caput apri defero
Reddens laudes Domino.

The boar's head in hand bring I,
With garlands gay and rosemary,
I pray you all sing merrily,
Qui estis in conuiuio.

The boar's head, I understand,
Is the chief service in this land.
Look wherever it be found,
Seruite cum cantico.

Be glad, lords, both more and less,
For this hath ordained our steward,
To cheer you all this Christmas,
The boar's head with mustard.

The Boar is Dead[2]

1607.

The boar is dead,
Lo, here is his head;
What man could have done more
Than his head off to strike
Meleager-like,
And bring it as I do before?

[1] Wynkyn de Worde, *Christmas Carolles.*
[2] *The Christmas Prince*, as given at St. John's College, Oxford.

The Boar is Dead

He living spoiled
Where good men toiled,
  Which made kind Ceres sorry;
But now dead and drawn,
Is very good brawn,
  And we have brought it for ye.

Then set down the swineyard,
The foe to the vineyard,
  Let Bacchus crown his fall;
Let this boar's head and mustard,
Stand for pig, goose, and custard,
  And so you are welcome all.

VENI CORONABERIS[1]

Holly and Ivy Made a Great Party

Fifteenth Century.

HOLLY and Ivy made a great party,[2]
Who should have the mastery,
In landës where they go.

Then spoke Holly, " I am free and jolly,
I will have the mastery,
In landës where we go."

Then spake Ivy, " I am lov'd and prov'd,
And I will have the mastery,
In landës where we go."

Then spake Holly, and set him down on his knee,
" I pray thee, gentle Ivy,
Say me no villainy,
In landës where we go."

Alleluia, alleluia, alleluia, now sing we

Fifteenth Century.

HERE comes holly that is so gent,
To please all men is his intent,
Alleluia.

[1] See note. [2] *Here*, division into parties, *i.e.* contention.

But, lord and lady of this hall,
Whosoever against holly call,
Alleluia,

Whosoever against holly do cry,
In a leap [1] shall he hang full high,
Alleluia.

Whosoever against holly do sing,
He may weep and his handës wring,
Alleluia.

Ivy chief of trees it is,
Veni coronaberis

Fifteenth Century.

The most worthy she is in town,
He that saith other, doth amiss;
And worthy to bear the crown;
Veni coronaberis.

Ivy is soft and meek of speech,
Against all bale she is bliss;
Well is he that may her reach;
Veni coronaberis.

Ivy is green, with colour bright,
Of all trees best she is;
And that I prove well now by right;
Veni coronaberis.

[1] Basket.

Ivy beareth berries black;
God grant us all His bliss!
For there shall me nothing lack,
Veni coronaberis.

A Song on the Ivy and the Holly

Temp. Henry VI.

Nay, ivy, nay, it shall not be, ywis,
Let holly have the mastery as the manner is.

HOLLY stands in the hall, fair to behold,
Ivy stands without the door, she is full sore a-cold.
Nay, ivy, nay, it shall not be, ywis,
Let holly have the mastery as the manner is.

Holly and his merry men they dancen and they sing,[1]
Ivy and her maidens they weepen and they wring.
Nay, ivy, nay, it shall not be, ywis,
Let holly have the mastery as the manner is.

Ivy hath a kibe,[2] she caught it with the cold;
So may they all have one, that with ivy hold.
Nay, ivy, nay, it shall not be, ywis,
Let holly have the mastery as the manner is.

Holly hath berries as red as any rose,
The forester, the hunters keep them fro the does.
Nay, ivy, nay, it shall not be, ywis,
Let holly have the mastery as the manner is.

[1] See note. [2] Chilblain.

Ivy hath berries as black as any sloes,
Then comes the owl and eats them as she goes.
Nay, ivy, nay, it shall not be, ywis,
Let holly have the mastery as the manner is.

Holly hath birdës a full fair flock,
The nightingale, the popinjay, the gentle laverock.
Nay, ivy, nay, it shall not be, ywis,
Let holly have the mastery as the manner is.

Good ivy, what birdës hast thou ?
None but the owlet that cries " How, how ! "
Nay, ivy, nay, it shall not be, ywis,
Let holly have the mastery as the manner is.

Nay, Nay, Ivy !

Before 1536.

Nay, nay, Ivy !
It may not be, ywis,
For Holly must have the mastery
As the manner is.

Holly beareth berries,
Berries red enough ;
The throstlecock, the popinjay
Dance in every bough.

Welaway, sorry Ivy !
What fowls hast thou
But the sorry owlet
That singeth " How, how ! " ?

Ivy beareth berries
  As black as any sloe,
There cometh the wood culver,
  And feedeth her of tho;[1]

She lifteth up her tail
  And she cakes ere she go;
She would not for an hundred pound
  Serve Holly so.

Holly with his merry men
  They can dance in hall;
Ivy and her gentle women
  Cannot dance at all,

But like a meiny of bullocks
  In a waterfall,
Or on a hot summer's day
  When they be mad all.

Holly and his merry men
  Sit in chairs of gold;
Ivy and her gentle women
  Sit without in fold, .

With a pair of kibëd[2]
  Heels caught with cold;
So would I that every man had
  That with Ivy will hold!

[1] Them. [2] With chilblains.

The Holly and the Ivy[1]

Traditional.

THE holly and the ivy
Now are both well grown;
Of all the trees that are in the wood
The holly bears the crown.
The rising of the sun,
The running of the deer,
The playing of the merry organ,
Sweet singing in the choir.

The holly bears a blossom
As white as lily flower;
And Mary bore sweet Jesus Christ,
To be our sweet Saviour.
The rising of the sun,
The running of the deer,
The playing of the merry organ,
Sweet singing in the choir.

The holly bears a berry,
As red as any blood;
And Mary bore sweet Jesus Christ
To do poor sinners good.
The rising of the sun,
The running of the deer,
The playing of the merry organ,
Sweet singing in the choir.

[1] Printed in a broadside as early as 1710.

The holly bears a prickle
As sharp as any thorn;
And Mary bore sweet Jesus Christ
On Christmas day in the morn.
The rising of the sun,
The running of the deer,
The playing of the merry organ,
Sweet singing in the choir.

The holly bears a bark
As bitter as any gall;
And Mary bore sweet Jesus Christ
For to redeem us all.
The rising of the sun,
The running of the deer,
The playing of the merry organ,
Sweet singing in the choir.

The holly and the ivy
Now are both well grown;
Of all the trees that are in the wood,
The holly bears the crown.
The rising of the sun,
The running of the deer,
The playing of the merry organ,
Sweet singing in the choir.

APPENDIX I

CHRISTMAS HYMNS AND OTHER LYRICS

For Christmas Day[1]

1576. Francis Kinwelmersh.

REJOICE, rejoice, with heart and voice!
In Christës birth this day rejoice!
From virgin's womb this day did spring
The precious seed that only savëd man:
This day let man rejoice and sweetly sing,
Since on this day salvation first began.
This day did Christ man's soul from death remove,
With glorious saints to dwell in heaven above.

This day to man came pledge of perfect peace,
This day to man came perfect unity,
This day man's grief began to surcease,
This day did man receive a remedy
For each offence and every deadly sin
With guilty heart that erst he wandered in.

In Christës flock let love be surely placed,
From Christës flock let concord hate expel,
Of Christës flock let love be so embraced
As we in Christ and Christ in us may dwell;
Christ is the author of all unity,
From whence proceedeth all felicity.

[1] *Paradise of Dainty Devices.*

The Burning Babe

1595. Robert Southwell.

As I in hoary winter's night stood shivering in the snow,
Surprised I was with sudden heat which made my heart to glow;

And lifting up a fearful eye to view what fire was near,
A pretty Babe all burning bright did in the air appear,

Who scorchëd with excessive heat such floods of tears did shed,
As though his floods should quench his flames which with his tears were fed.

"Alas!" quoth he, "but newly born in fiery heats I fry,
Yet none approach to warm their hearts or feel my fire but I!

My faultless heart the furnace is, the fuel wounding thorns;
Love is the fire and sighs the smoke, the ashes shame and scorns;

The fuel Justice layeth on, and Mercy blows the coals;
The metal in this furnace wrought are men's defilëd souls;

For which, as now on fire I am, to work them to their good,
So will I melt into a bath to wash them in my blood."

With that he vanished out of sight and swiftly shrunk away,
And straightway I called into mind that it was Christmas Day.

New Prince, New Pomp

1595. Robert Southwell.

Behold a silly tender Babe,
In freezing winter night,
In homely manger trembling lies;
Alas, a piteous sight.

The inns are full, no man will yield
This little pilgrim bed;
But forced He is with silly beasts
In crib to shroud His head.

Despise Him not for lying there,
First what He is inquire;
An orient pearl is often found
In depth of dirty mire.

Weigh not His crib, His wooden dish,
Nor beast that by Him feed;
Weigh not His mother's poor attire,
Nor Joseph's simple weed.

This stable is a Prince's court,
This crib His chair of state;
The beasts are parcel of His pomp,
The wooden dish His plate.

The persons in that poor attire
His royal liveries wear;
The Prince Himself is come from heaven,
This pomp is praisëd there,

With joy approach, O Christian wight!
Do homage to thy King;
And highly praise this humble pomp
Which He from heaven doth bring.

A Hymn on the Nativity of my Saviour

1573 (?)-1637. Ben Jonson.

I SING the birth was born to-night,
The Author both of life and light;
The angels so did sound it.
And like the ravished shepherds said,
Who saw the light and were afraid,
Yet searched, and true they found it.

The Son of God, th' eternal King,
That did us all salvation bring,
And freed the soul from danger;
He whom the whole world could not take,
The Word, which heaven and earth did make,
Was now laid in a manger.

The Father's wisdom willed it so,
The Son's obedience knew no No,
Both wills were in one stature;
And as that wisdom had decreed,
The Word was now made flesh indeed,
And took on Him our nature.

What comfort by Him do we win,
Who made Himself the price of sin,
To make us heirs of glory!
To see this Babe all innocence;
A Martyr born in our defence;
Can man forget the story?

The Angels

1585–1649. William Drummond of Hawthornden.

RUN, shepherds, run where Bethlehem blest appears.
We bring the best of news; be not dismayed;
A Saviour there is born more old than years,
Amidst heaven's rolling height this earth who stayed.
In a poor cottage inned, a virgin maid
A weakling did Him bear, who all upbears;
There is He poorly swaddled, in manger laid,
To whom too narrow swaddlings are our spheres;
Run, shepherds, run and solemnise his birth.
This is that night—no, day grown great with bliss,
In which the power of Satan broken is:
In heaven be glory, peace unto the earth!
Thus singing, through the air the angels swam,
And cope of stars reëchoed the same.

Who can Forget—Never to be Forgot

1588–1623. Giles Fletcher.

WHO can forget—never to be forgot—
The time, that all the world in slumber lies,
When like the stars the singing angels shot
To earth, and heaven awakëd all his eyes,
To see another sun at midnight rise
On earth? Was ever sight of pareil fame
For God before, man like Himself did frame,
But God Himself now like a mortal was became.

A Child He was, and had not learnt to speak,
That with His word the world before did make.
His mother's arms Him bore, He was so weak,
That with one hand the vaults of heaven could shake.

See how small room my infant Lord doth take
    Whom all the world is not enough to hold,
    Who of His years, as of His age hath told ?
Never such age so young, never a child so old.

And yet but newly He was infanted,
  And yet already He was sought to die ;
Yet scarcely born, already banishëd.
  Not able yet to go, and forced to fly :
But scarcely fled away, when by and by,
    The tyran's[1] sword with blood is all defiled,
    And Rachel, for her sons, with fury wild,
Cries, " O thou cruel king, and O my sweetest child ! "

Egypt His nurse became, where Nilus springs,
  Who, straight to entertain the rising sun,
The hasty harvest in his bosom brings ;[2]
  But now for drought the fields were all undone,
And now with waters all is overrun :
    So fast the Cynthian mountains poured their snow,
    When once they felt the sun so near them glow,
That Nilus Egypt lost, and to sea did grow.

The angels carolled loud their song of peace ;
  The cursëd oracles were strucken dumb ;
To see their Shepherd the poor shepherds press ;
  To see their kneeling the kingly sophies[3] come ;
And them to guide unto his Master's home,
    A star comes dancing up the Orient,
    That springs for joy over the strawy tent,
Where gold to make their prince a crown, they all present.

1 Tyrant. 2 Cf. *The Carnal and the Crane.* 3 Wise men.

Christmas [1]

1593–1633. George Herbert.

All after pleasures as I rode one day,
  My horse and I both tired, body and mind,
With full cry of affections quite astray,
  I took up in the next inn I could find.

There, when I came, whom found I but my dear—
  My dearest Lord; expecting till the grief
Of pleasures brought me to Him, ready there
  To be all passengers' most sweet relief?

O Thou, whose glorious yet contracted light
  Wrapt in night's mantle, stole into a manger;
Since my dark soul and brutish is Thy right,
  To man, of all beasts be not Thou a stranger;

Furnish and deck my soul, that Thou mayst have
A better lodging than a rack or grave.
The shepherds sing; and shall I silent be?
  My God, no hymn for Thee?
My soul's a shepherd too; a flock it feeds
  Of thoughts and words and deeds.
The pasture is Thy word, the streams Thy grace,
  Enriching every place.

Shepherd and flock shall sing, and all my powers
  Outsing the daylight hours.
Then we will chide the sun for letting night
  Take up his place and right:
We sing one common Lord; wherefore He should
  Himself the candle hold.

[1] *The Temple.*

I will go searching till I find a sun
  Shall stay till we have done;
A willing shiner, that shall shine as gladly
  As frost-nipt suns look sadly.
Then we will sing and shine all our own day,
  And one another pay.
His beams shall cheer my heart, and both so twine,
Till e'en his beams sing and my music shine.

An Ode on the Birth of our Saviour [1]

1647. Robert Herrick.

In numbers, and but these few,
I sing Thy birth, O Jesu!
Thou pretty baby, born here
With superabundant scorn here:
Who for Thy princely port here,
    Hadst for Thy place
    Of birth, a base
Outstable for Thy court here.

Instead of neat enclosures
Of interwoven osiers,
Instead of fragrant posies
Of daffodils and roses,
Thy cradle, Kingly Stranger,
    As gospel tells,
    Was nothing else
But here a homely manger.

But we with silks not crewels,
With sundry precious jewels,
And lily-work will dress Thee;

[1] *Noble Numbers.*

And, as we dispossess Thee
Of clouts, we'll make a chamber,
Sweet babe, for Thee
Of ivory,
And plaster'd round with amber.

The Jews they did disdain Thee,
But we will entertain Thee
With glories to await here
Upon Thy princely state here;
And, more for love than pity,
From year to year
We'll make Thee here
A free-born of our city.

The Wassail[1]

1648.

Robert Herrick

Give way, give way, ye gates, and win
An easy blessing to your bin
And basket by our entering in.

May both with manchet stand replete;
Your larders too so hung with meat
That, though a thousand thousand eat,

Yet, ere twelve moons shall whirl about
Their silvery spheres, there's none may doubt
But more's sent in than was serv'd out.

Next may your dairies prosper so
As that your pans no ebb may know;
But if they do, the more to flow,

[1] *Hesperides.*

Like to a solemn sober stream,
  Bank'd all with lilies and the cream
Of sweetest cowslips filling them.

Then may your plants be pressed with fruit,
  Nor bee or hive you have be mute,
But sweetly sounding like a lute.

Next may your ducks and teeming-hen
  Both to the cock's tread say Amen,
And for their two eggs render ten.

Last may your harrows, shares and ploughs,
  Your stacks, your stocks, your sweetest mows,
All prosper by your virgin vows.

Alas! we bless, but see none here
  That brings us either ale or beer:
In a dry house all things are near.

Let's leave a longer time to wait,
  When rust and cobwebs bind the gate
And all live here with needy Fate.

Where chimneys do forever weep
  For want of warmth, and stomachs keep
With noise the servants' eyes from sleep.

It is in vain to sing or stay
  Our free feet here; but we'll away:
Yet to the Lares this we'll say—

The time will come when you'll be sad
  And reckon this for fortune had,
T'have lost the good ye might have had.

The Shepherds [1]

1650-1665. Henry Vaughan.

Sweet, harmless livers! on whose holy leisure
Waits innocence and pleasure;
Whose leaders to those pastures and clear springs
Were patriarchs, saints and kings;
How happened it that in the dead of night
You only saw true light,
While Palestine was fast asleep and lay
Without one thought of day?
Was it because those first and blessed swains
Were pilgrims on those plains
When they received the promise, for which now
'Twas then first shown to you?

'Tis true He loves that dust whereon they go
That serve Him here below,
And therefore might for memory of those
His love there first disclose;
But wretched Salem, once His love, must now
No voice nor vision know;
Here stately piles with all their height and pride
Now languished and died,
And Bethlehem's humble cots above them stept
While all her seers slept;
Her cedar fir, hewed stones, and gold were all
Polluted through their fall;
And those once sacred mansions were now
Mere emptiness and show.

[1] *Silex Scintillans.*

This made the angel call at reeds and thatch,
  Yet where the shepherds watch,
And God's own lodging, though He could not lack,
  To be a common rack.
No costly pride, no soft-clothed luxury
  In those thin cells could lie;
Each stirring wind and storm blew through their cots,
  Which never harboured plots;
Only content and love and humble joys
  Lived there without all noise;
Perhaps some harmless cares for the next day
  Did in their bosoms play,
As where to lead their ship,[1] what silent nook,
  What springs or shades to look;
But that was all; and now with gladsome care
  They for the town prepare;
They leave their flock, and in a busy talk
  All towards Bethlem walk,
To seek their soul's great Shepherd who was come
  To bring all stragglers home;
Where now they find Him out, and, taught before,
  That Lamb of God adore,
That Lamb, whose days great kings and prophets wished
  And longed to see, but missed.
The first light they beheld was bright and gay,
  And turned their night to day;
But to this later light they saw in Him
  This day was dark and dim.

[1] Sheep.

A Rocking Hymn [1]

1588–1667. George Wither.

SWEET baby, sleep; what ails my dear?
What ails my darling thus to cry?
Be still, my child, and lend thine ear
To hear me sing thy lullaby.
My pretty lamb, forbear to weep;
Be still, my dear; sweet baby, sleep.

Thou blessed soul, what canst thou fear?
What thing to thee can mischief do?
Thy God is now thy father dear;
His holy spouse thy mother too.
Sweet baby, then, forbear to weep;
Be still, my babe; sweet baby, sleep.

Whilst thus thy lullaby I sing,
For thee great blessings ripening be;
Thine eldest brother is a king,
And hath a kingdom bought for thee.
Sweet baby, then, forbear to weep;
Be still, my babe; sweet baby, sleep.

Sweet baby, sleep, and nothing fear,
For whosoever thee offends,
By thy protector threatened are,
And God and angels are thy friends.
Sweet baby, then, forbear to weep,
Be still, my babe; sweet baby, sleep.

[1] *Hallelujah, or Britain's Sacred Remembrancer.*

When God with us was dwelling here,
  In little babes he took delight:
Such innocents as then, my dear,
  Are ever precious in his sight.
    Sweet baby, then, forbear to weep,
    Be still, my babe; sweet baby, sleep.

A little infant once was he,
  And Strength-in-Weakness then was laid
Upon his virgin-mother's knee,
  That power to thee might be conveyed.
    Sweet baby, then, forbear to weep;
    Be still, my babe; sweet baby, sleep.

In this thy frailty and thy need
  He friends and helpers doth prepare,
Which thee shall cherish, clothe and feed,
  For of thy weal they tender are.
    Sweet baby, then, forbear to weep;
    Be still, my babe; sweet baby, sleep.

The King of kings when he was born,
  Had not so much for outward ease;
By him such dressings were not worn,
  Nor suchlike swaddling-clothes as these.
    Sweet baby, then, forbear to weep;
    Be still, my babe; sweet baby, sleep.

Within a manger lodged thy Lord,
  Where oxen lay and asses fed;
Warm rooms we do to thee afford,
  An easy cradle or a bed.
    Sweet baby, then, forbear to weep;
    Be still, my babe; sweet baby, sleep.

The wants that He did then sustain
  Have purchased wealth, my babe, for thee,
And by His torments and His pain
  Thy rest and ease securëd be.
    My baby, then, forbear to weep;
    Be still, my babe; sweet baby, sleep.

Thou hast (yet more), to perfect this,
  A promise and an earnest got
Of gaining everlasting bliss,
  Though thou, my babe, perceiv'st it not.
    Sweet baby, then, forbear to weep;
    Be still, my babe; sweet baby, sleep.

On the Infancy of our Saviour[1]

1592–1644. Francis Quarles.

Hail, blessed virgin, full of heavenly grace,
Blest above all that sprang from human race;
Whose heav'n-saluted womb brought forth in one,
A blessed Saviour and a blessed Son:
O! what a ravishment 't had been to see
Thy little Saviour perking on thy knee!
To see Him nuzzle in thy virgin breast
His milk-white body all unclad, all undressed!
To see thy busy fingers clothe and wrap
His spraddling limbs in thy indulgent lap!
To see His desperate eyes, with childish grace,
Smiling upon His smiling mother's face!

[1] *Divine Fancies.*

And when His forward strength began to bloom,
To see Him diddle up and down the room!
O, who would think so sweet a Babe as this,
Should e'er be slain by a false-hearted kiss!
Had I a rag, if sure Thy body wore it,
Pardon, sweet Babe, I think I should adore it.
Till then, O grant this boon (a boon far dearer),
The weed not being, I may adore the wearer.

Hymn for Christmas Day [1]

BEING A DIALOGUE BETWEEN THREE SHEPHERDS

1613–1667. Jeremy Taylor.

Where is this blessed Babe
That hath made
All the world so full of joy
And expectation;
That glorious Boy
That crowns each nation
With a triumphant wreath of blessedness?

Where should He be but in the throng,
And among
His angel ministers that sing
And take wing
Just as may echo to His voice,
And rejoice
When wing and tongue and all
May so procure their happiness?

[1] *Festival Hymns.*

But He hath other waiters now:
A poor cow,
An ox and mule, stand and behold,
And wonder
That a stable should enfold
Him that can thunder.

Chorus. O what a gracious God have we,
How good! how great! even as our misery.

A Hymn for Christmas Day[1]

1613–1667. Jeremy Taylor.

AWAKE, my soul, and come away.
Put on thy best array;
Lest if thou longer stay
Thou lose some minutes of so blest a day.
Go run
And bid good-morrow to the sun;
Welcome his safe return
To Capricorn.
And that great morn
Wherein a God was born,
Whose story none can tell
But He whose every word's a miracle.

To-day Almightiness grew weak.
The Word itself was mute and could not speak.

That Jacob's star which made the sun
To dazzle if he durst look on,
Now mantled o'er in Bethlehem's night,
Borrowed a star to show him light.

[1] *Festival Hymns.*

He that begirt each zone,
To whom both poles are one,
Who grasped the Zodiac in His hand
And made it move or stand,
Is now by nature man,
By stature but a span;
Eternity is now grown short;
A king is born without a court;
The water thirsts; the fountain's dry;
And life, being born, made apt to die.

Chorus. Then let our praises emulate and vie
With His humility!
Since He's exiled from the skies
That we might rise—
From low estate of men
Let's sing Him up again!
Each man wind up his heart
To bear a part
In that angelic choir and show
His glory high as He was low.
Let's sing towards men goodwill and charity,
Peace upon earth, glory to God on high!
Hallelujah! Hallelujah!

APPENDIX II

MODERN CAROLS IN THE MEDIEVAL MANNER

Modryb Marya—Aunt Mary

A CHRISTMAS CHANT

1838. Robert Stephen Hawker.

Now, of all the trees by the king's highway,
  Which do you love the best?
O! the one that is green upon Christmas Day,
  The bush with the bleeding breast.
Now the holly with her drops of blood for me:
For that is our dear Aunt Mary's tree.

Its leaves are sweet with our Saviour's Name,
  'Tis a plant that loves the poor:
Summer and winter it shines the same
  Beside the cottage door.
O! the holly with her drops of blood for me:
For that is our kind Aunt Mary's tree.

'Tis a bush that the birds will never leave:
  They sing in it all day long;
But sweetest of all upon Christmas Eve
  Is to hear the robin's song.
'Tis the merriest sound upon earth and sea:
For it comes from our own Aunt Mary's tree.

So, of all that grow by the king's highway,
  I love that tree the best;
'Tis a bower for the birds upon Christmas Day,
  The bush of the bleeding breast.
O! the holly with her drops of blood for me:
For that is our sweet Aunt Mary's tree.

The Virgin's Cradle-Hymn [1]

1817. S. T. Coleridge.

DORMI, Jesu! Mater ridet
Quae tam dulcem somnum videt,
  Dormi, Jesu! blandule!
Si non dormis, Mater plorat,
Inter fila cantans orat,
  Blande, veni, somnule.

English

Sleep, sweet babe! my cares beguiling:
Mother sits beside thee smiling;
  Sleep, my darling, tenderly!
If thou sleep not, mother mourneth,
Singing as her wheel she turneth:
  Come, soft slumber, balmily!

Masters, in this Hall

1860. William Morris.

"To Bethlem did they go, the shepherds three;
To Bethlem did they go to see whe'r it were so or no,
  Whether Christ were born or no
    To set men free."

[1] *Sibylline Leaves.*

Masters in this Hall,
  Hear ye news to-day
Brought from over sea,
  And ever I you pray.

CHORUS.

Nowell! Nowell! Nowell!
    Nowell sing we clear!
Holpen are all folk on earth,
    Born is GOD'S son so dear:
Nowell! Nowell! Nowell!
  Nowell sing we loud!
GOD to-day hath poor folk rais'd,
  And cast adown the proud.

Going over the hills,
  Through the milk-white snow,
Heard I ewes bleat
  While the wind did blow.
    Chorus.—Nowell, &c.

Shepherds many an one
  Sat among the sheep,
No man spake more word
  Than they had been asleep.
    Chorus.—Nowell, &c.

Quoth I, "Fellows mine,
  Why this guise sit ye?
Making but dull cheer,
  Shepherds though ye be?
    Chorus.—Nowell, &c.

"Shepherds should of right
  Leap and dance and sing,
Thus to see ye sit
  Is a right strange thing."
    Chorus.—Nowell, &c.

Quoth these fellows then,
  "To Bethlem town we go,
To see a Mighty LORD
  Lie in manger low."
    Chorus.—Nowell, &c.

"How name ye this LORD,
  Shepherds?" then said I,
"Very GOD," they said,
  "Come from Heaven high."
    Chorus.—Nowell, &c.

Then to Bethlem town
  We went two and two,
And in a sorry place
  Heard the oxen low.
    Chorus.—Nowell, &c.

Therein did we see
  A sweet and godly May,
And a fair old man,
  Upon the straw She lay.
    Chorus.—Nowell, &c.

And a little CHILD
  On Her arm had She;
"Wot ye Who This is?"
  Said the hinds to me.
    Chorus.—Nowell, &c.

Ox and ass Him know,
 Kneeling on their knee,
Wondrous joy had I
 This little Babe to see.
 Chorus.—Nowell, &c.

This is Christ the Lord,
 Masters be ye glad!
Christmas is come in,
 And no folk should be sad.
 Chorus.—Nowell, &c.

Outlanders, Whence Come ye Last?[1]

William Morris.

Outlanders, whence come ye last?
 The snow in the street and the wind on the door.
Through what green sea and great have ye passed?
 Minstrels and maids, stand forth on the floor.

From far away, O masters mine,
 The snow in the street and the wind on the door.
We come to bear you goodly wine,
 Minstrels and maids, stand forth on the floor.

From far away we come to you,
 The snow in the street and the wind on the door.
To tell of great tidings strange and true.
 Minstrels and maids, stand forth on the floor.

[1] *The Earthly Paradise*, printed here by kind permission of William Morris's trustees and of Messrs. Longmans, Green and Co.

News, news of the Trinity,
The snow in the street and the wind on the door.
And Mary and Joseph from over the sea!
Minstrels and maids, stand forth on the floor.

For as we wandered far and wide,
The snow in the street and the wind on the door
What hap do ye deem there should us betide!
Minstrels and maids, stand forth on the floor.

Under a bent when the night was deep,
The snow in the street and the wind on the door.
There lay three shepherds tending their sheep.
Minstrels and maids, stand forth on the floor.

"O ye shepherds, what have ye seen,
The snow in the street and the wind on the door.
To slay your sorrow and heal your teen?"
Minstrels and maids, stand forth on the floor.

"In an ox-stall this night we saw,
The snow in the street and the wind on the door.
A babe and a maid without a flaw.
Minstrels and maids, stand forth on the floor.

"There was an old man there beside,
The snow in the street and the wind on the door.
His hair was white and his hood was wide.
Minstrels and maids, stand forth on the floor.

"And as we gazed this thing upon,
The snow in the street and the wind on the door.
Those twain knelt down to the Little One.
Minstrels and maids, stand forth on the floor.

"And a marvellous song we straight did hear,
The snow in the street and the wind on the door.
That slew our sorrow and healed our care."
Minstrels and maids, stand forth on the floor.

News of a fair and a marvellous thing,
The snow in the street and the wind on the door.
Nowell, nowell, nowell, we sing!
Minstrels and maids, stand forth on the floor.

A Christmas Carol [1]

Christina G. Rossetti.

IN the bleak mid-winter
Frosty wind made moan,
Earth stood hard as iron,
Water like a stone;
Snow had fallen, snow on snow,
Snow on snow,
In the bleak mid-winter
Long ago.

Our God, heaven cannot hold Him,
Nor earth sustain;
Heaven and earth shall flee away
When He comes to reign:
In the bleak mid-winter
A stable-place sufficed
The Lord God Almighty,
Jesus Christ.

[1] Printed here by kind permission of Messrs. Macmillan and Co.

Enough for Him whom cherubim
  Worship night and day,
A breastful of milk
  And a mangerful of hay;
Enough for Him whom angels
  Fall down before,
The ox and ass and camel
  Which adore.

Angels and archangels
  May have gathered there,
Cherubim and seraphim
  Throng'd the air,
But only His mother
  In her maiden bliss
Worshipped the Beloved
  With a kiss.

What can I give Him,
  Poor as I am?
If I were a shepherd
  I would bring a lamb,
If I were a wise man
  I would do my part,—
Yet what I can I give Him,
    Give my heart.

Three Damsels in the Queen's Chamber [1]

1866.

A. C. Swinburne.

Three damsels in the queen's chamber,
The queen's mouth was most fair;
She spake a word of God's mother
As the combs went in her hair.
Mary that is of might,
Bring us to thy Son's sight.

They held the gold combs out from her,
A span's length off her head;
She sang this song of God's mother
And of her bearing-bed.
Mary most full of grace,
Bring us to thy Son's face.

When she sat at Joseph's hand,
She looked against her side;
And either way from the short silk band
Her girdle was all wried.
Mary that all good may,
Bring us to thy Son's way.

Mary had three women for her bed,
The twain were maidens clean;
The first of them had white and red,
The third had riven green.
Mary that is so sweet,
Bring us to thy Son's feet.

[1] *Poems and Ballads. First Series.* Printed here by kind permission of Mr. Theodore Watts-Dunton.

She had three women for her hair,
  Two were gloved soft and shod;
The third had feet and fingers bare,
  She was the likest God.
    Mary that wieldeth land,
    Bring us to thy Son's hand.

She had three women for her ease,
  The twain were good women:
The first two were the two Maries,
  The third was Magdalen.
    Mary that perfect is,
    Bring us to thy Son's kiss.

Joseph had three workmen in his stall,
  To serve him well upon;
The first of them were Peter and Paul,
  The third of them was John.
    Mary, God's handmaiden,
    Bring us to thy Son's ken.

" If your child be none other man's,
  But if it be very mine,
The bedstead shall be gold two spans,
  The bedfoot silver fine."
    Mary that made God mirth,
    Bring us to thy Son's birth.

" If the child be some other man's,
  And if it be none of mine,
The manger shall be straw two spans,
  Betwixen kine and kine."
    Mary that made sin cease,
    Bring us to thy Son's peace

Christ was born upon this wise,
  It fell on such a night,
Neither with sounds of psalteries,
  Nor with fire for light.
    Mary that is God's spouse,
    Bring us to thy Son's house.

The star came out upon the east
  With a great sound and sweet:
Kings gave gold to make him feast
  And myrrh for him to eat.
    Mary, of thy sweet mood,
    Bring us to thy Son's good.

He had two handmaids at his head,
  One handmaid at his feet;
The twain of them were fair and red,
  The third one was right sweet.
    Mary that is most wise,
    Bring us to thy Son's eyes. Amen.

A Christmas Lullaby[1]

1840-93. John Addington Symonds.

SLEEP, baby, sleep! The Mother sings:
Heaven's angels kneel and fold their wings.
    Sleep, baby, sleep!

With swathes of scented hay thy bed
By Mary's hand at eve was spread.
    Sleep, baby, sleep!

[1] Printed here by kind permission of Mr. Horatio F. Brown.

At midnight came the shepherds, they
Whom seraphs wakened by the way.
Sleep, baby, sleep!

And three kings from the east afar
Ere dawn came guided by thy star.
Sleep, baby, sleep!

They brought thee gifts of gold and gems,
Pure orient pearls, rich diadems.
Sleep, baby, sleep!

But thou who liest slumbering there,
Art King of kings, earth, ocean, air.
Sleep, baby, sleep!

Sleep, baby, sleep! The shepherds sing:
Through heaven, through earth, hosannas ring.
Sleep, baby, sleep!

NOTES

P. 159. *Mirabile Misterium*. The title carol is written on a blank leaf of an imperfect tract printed by Wynkyn de Worde, and is singular in its personification of abstract qualities such as occur in the morality plays. The carols in this group show more orthodoxy and piety than originality or poetry. They are difficult to distinguish from other groups, because they usually include some details of the Nativity and frequently merge into the songs of Christmas joy.

P. 160. *Awdlay*, or Audelay. A blind and deaf monk, chaplain in Haughmond Abbey, Shropshire.

P. 164. *Blessed be the time*, &c. The logic is that Eve by her sin made redemption possible through Mary. Cf. the next three carols; also Part I. p. 30, *Ave fit ex Eva.*

P. 181. *Richard Smert*, or Smart. Various compositions in the Fairfax MS. are attributed to this man, who was said to be of Plymtree (Devonshire). He sometimes collaborated with John Trouluffe, or Truelove (cf. p. 183), but whether they were responsible for words as well as music is uncertain. The carols on pp. 181–183 show strong resemblances.

P. 186. *A blessed bird*, &c. The word *bird*, meaning son, young man, was in use chiefly between 1300 and 1571.

With the exception of the first line this carol has nothing to do with Christmas and might be included in Appendix II. The idea underlying the symbolism is of the Host.

P. 193. *Lully, lulley*, &c. This carol, of which the one following is a modern version, is interesting as showing the persistence of a lyric for four hundred years (the first version is probably of the fifteenth century, the second was taken from the recital of a boy who came with morris-dancers some years before 1862, cf. *Notes and Queries*, third series, ii. p. 103); and also because it seems to have been suggested by some form of the legend of the Holy Grail. The Bleeding Knight is Christ, the "may" is His mother, the "falcon" is introduced apparently to suggest that the body of the poem is a vision. It is interesting to note that the modern version is the more specific of the two, adding the hound which licks the blood (the Church?) and the Holy Thorn of Glastonbury, which is intimately associated with the Grail story.

P. 195. *Remember, O Thou Man.* A didactic religious poem, included by John Wedderburn in his *Compendious Buik*, seems to be a parody of this, which is therefore probably older than 1567.

P. 201. *The Moon shone bright.* According to Husk this has the repute of having been sung by the bellman or watchman making his rounds. Its content certainly bears out this character; and although it contains much that is fairly modern, it may have developed from an earlier poem. Cf. Shakespeare, *As You Like It* (Act v. sc. 4), where in the poem "It was a lover and his lass," the lines—

> "This carol they began that hour
> How that life was but a flower," &c.

may possibly be reminiscent of some version of this.

P. 203. *In Dulci Iubilo.* I have distinguished the few carols that dwell upon the more spiritual side of Christmas joy from those in which the enjoyment of material things is emphasized.

P. 209. *All the merrier*, &c. The symbolism of the "sun of grace" is carried through the chief divisions of the day—prime, noon and undern.

P. 209. *Him shineth. Him* seems to refer to Christ, although this interpretation is not without difficulties. The verb is *schynit*, which should be properly *shineth;* but the other verbs are all in the past tense.

P. 217. *Carols of Festivity.* This heading includes several carols of welcome and general good cheer, special carols that herald the bringing in of the boar's head, wassail songs, and the decoration of the hall with ivy and holly. The religious element is touched upon but lightly, and the atmosphere is of pagan revelry, particularly noticeable in the examples belonging to the seventeenth century.

P. 217. *Proface.* These carols usually suggest the background of lavish hospitality, sometimes from the point of view of the givers, again of the seekers.

P. 243. *Wassail.* The oldest carol known (cf. Appendix I. p. 132), although Anglo-Norman, embodies the Saxon phrases used in pledging. The former of these has survived in the refrain of the initial carol of this group, which is otherwise highly religious. In the seventeenth century the wassail was a definite institution—the carrying about of a bowl of spiced ale from house to house to drink healths in expectation of a contribution. Nowadays the utterance of a "Merry Christmas" is often judged sufficient for the tip. Some of the poems here included are mere drinking-songs, but they were probably sung as carols at Christmas.

P. 245. *Bring us in good ale,* &c. In the MS. this song is preceded by the carol beginning,

> "Nowell, nowell, nowell,
> This is the salutation of the angel Gabriel"

(cf. Part I. p. 35) and the note: "This is the tune for the song following; if so be that ye will have another tune, it may be at your pleasure, for I have set all the song."

P. 255. *As I sat under a sycamore tree.* This carol, with its variant *As I sat on a sunny bank,* is still popular in various parts of England. Another version, minus the wassail element, is given on p. 213. The conception of Mary and Christ as sailing in a ship is very old; I have seen it in a stone carving taken from a chimney-piece of about the year 1500.

P. 256. *Caput Apri Defero.* The boar's-head carols are interesting as embodying a ceremony surviving from a pagan sacrificial feast. Numerous as are the versions, their general effect is strikingly similar. Two give an account of the killing of the beast, and one drags in Christian symbolism by comparing him to Christ.

P. 258. *The second course.* All these things are mentioned in cookery books and directions for carving between the days of Henry IV. and James I. Some of them, as bruet of Allmayne and frumenty, were especially associated with Christmas cheer.

P. 262. *Veni coronaberis.* The holly and ivy carols exist in various forms and in many MSS. The singing of them seems to be a survival of some sort of Nature-worship. The two plants most characteristic of the season of the year seem to have been impersonated—holly by young men, ivy by maidens; and the poems are regularly in the form of a debate or contention as to the respective merits of each. Perhaps in the decoration of the hall the work was so apportioned, and possibly there was earlier some sort of rude drama or dance connected with the ceremony. In the *Gentleman's Magazine* for 1779, p. 137, is mentioned a Shrovetide custom in East Kent which illustrates this old contention. The girls of a village burn a "Holly Boy" stolen from the boys; and the boys an "Ivy Girl" stolen from the girls, each in different parts of the village. The root idea seems to be whether the master or the mistress shall rule the household. Sandys in his *Christmas Carols* (1833, p. cxxii) tells a story that likewise associates this idea with Christmas. An old knight, while his guests were at table, asked that a carol be sung by the men who ruled their wives, and there was but a feeble response; but when he called upon the women who ruled their husbands, they fell all to such a singing that there was never heard such a caterwauling piece of music.

GLOSSARY

Adesto nunc propicius.	Be now propitious.
Agnoscat omne seculum.	Let all the world acknowledge Thee.
Alleluia.	Hallelujah.
Alma Redemptoris mater.	Dear mother of the Redeemer.
Alma beata Trinitas.	Dear blessed Trinity.
Amice Christi, Johannes.	John, Christ's friend.
A Patre Unigenitus.	The only Son of the Father.
Armati sunt perimentes.	The armed men are slaying.
A solis ortus cardine.	Arisen from the quarter of the sun.
Atque semper virgo.	And virgin ever.
Aurora lucis rutilat.	The dawn of light reddens.
Aurum, tus, myrram offerent.	They shall offer gold, frankincense and myrrh.
Ave Maria.	Hail, Mary !
Ave maris stella.	Hail, star of the sea.
Benedicamus Domino.	Let us bless the Lord.
Bevvex bien par tutte la company.	Drink well, all the company.
Bona natalicia.	Happy birthday feast.
Bona voluntaria.	Blessed offering.
Caput apri defero.	I bring the boar's head.
Celis tesaurizare.	To heap up treasures in the heavens.
Christe, Redemptor omnium.	Christ, the Redeemer of all.
Christo paremus canticam, excelsis gloria.	Let us prepare a song to Christ, glory on high.

Christus natus est.	Christ is born.
Circumfultus undique.	Shone upon from all sides.
Claro David germine.	Of the illustrious race of David.
Conditor alme siderum.	O blessed Founder of the stars.
Circumfuso sanguine.	With the shedding of blood.
Congaudere mihi.	To rejoice with me.
Consolamini.	Ye are consoled.
Consors Paterni luminis.	Consort of the light of the Father.
Constanter.	Steadfastly.
Contra regis consilia.	Contrary to the king's counsels.
Corpus Christi.	The Body of Christ.
Cum magna injuria.	With great injury.
Cum pudoris lilio.	With the lily of chastity.
Cum sua malicia	With their wickedness.
Cum sua potencia.	With his power.
Cum venerit judicare.	When He shall come to judge.
Cunctis reparatrix.	Renewer (fem.) of all things.
De fructu ventris.	Of the fruit of the womb.
Dei mater alma.	Gentle mother of God.
Demonis potencia.	By the power of the devil.
Deo gracias.	Thanks to God.
Deo Patri sit gloria.	Glory be to God the Father.
De te, genetrice.	Of thee, His mother.
Deus homo natus est.	God is born man.
De virgine Maria.	Of the virgin Mary.
De virgine purica.	Of a virgin most pure.
Dicam vobis quia.	I shall tell you wherefore.
Dieus wous garde, bewe sieurs.	God keep you, gentlemen.
Digno Tu (Te ?) scandente.	Thou fitly ascending.
Dolore.	With sorrow.
Dono cœlestis gratiæ.	With the gift of heavenly grace.
Ecce ancilla Domini.	Lo, the handmaid of the Lord.
Ecce sum humilima ancilla Domini.	I am the most humble handmaid of the Lord.
Ego dixi.	I have said.
Eia, Iesus hodie.	Lo, Jesus to-day.
Eia, martyr Stephane.	Lo, Stephen the martyr.

Enixa est puerpera.	The woman in childbed is delivered.
Et dixit: "Maria ne timeas,"	And said: "Mary, fear not."
Eterna Lux credencium.	Eternal Light of believers
Eterne Rex altissime.	O eternal King on high.
Et Princeps gloriae.	And Prince of glory.
Eva peccatrice.	By sinful Eve.
Exortum est.	He arose (*lit.* it has arisen).
Exultet celum laudibus.	Let heaven rejoice with praises.
Felix celi porta.	Blessed gate of heaven.
Felix fecundata.	Blessed in thy fertility.
Ferens mortis tedia.	Bearing the burden of death.
Ferventes insania.	Raging in their madness.
Fervore.	With raging.
Fervore gentis impiae.	By the rage of a wicked race.
Fraudenter.	Deceitfully.
Fulget Resurreccio.	The Resurrection shineth.
Gabriele nuncio.	From Gabriel the messenger.
Gaudeamus.	Let us rejoice.
Gentibus in Judæa.	Among the tribes in Judea.
Gloria in excelsis (Deo).	Glory on high (to God).
Gloria Tibi.	Glory to Thee.
Gloria Tibi, Domine.	Glory to Thee, O Lord.
Gracia Divina.	By Divine grace.
Hic erit Altissimi Filius.	He shall be the Son of the Most High.
Hostis Herodes impie.	O Herod, impious foe.
Iam lucis orto sidere.	Now the star of light having risen.
Iam ortus solis cardine.	Now arisen from the quarter of the sun.
Illaque favente.	By her favour.
In celi palacio.	In the palace of heaven.
In die Nativitatis.	On the day of the Nativity.
In die novissima.	On the last day.
In dulci iubilo.	In a sweet song of joy.
In excelsis gloria.	Glory on high.

Infans quem lactasti.	The Child whom thou hast suckled.
Infantis.	Of the Child.
Infantum festa colentes.	Keeping the feast of the Children.
Innixum Patris dextere.	Set on the right hand of the Father.
In praesepio.	In the manger.
In quo Christus natus est.	On which Christ was born.
In quo Salvator natus est.	On which the Saviour was born.
In Regis curia.	In the king's palace.
In reginensi atrio.	In the royal hall.
In sua malicia.	In their malice.
Jesu, Fili Dei.	Jesus, Son of God.
Jesu, Fili virginis.	Jesus, Son of the virgin.
Jesu, Salvator seculi.	Jesus, Saviour of the world.
Jesum semper amare.	To love Jesus always.
Johannes, Christi care.	John, Christ's beloved.
Kirieleyson.	Lord, have pity.
Lapidaverunt Stephanum.	They stoned Stephen.
Laudamus Te Dominum.	We praise Thee as Lord.
Laus Tibi.	Praise to Thee.
Laus Tibi sit gloria	Praise be to Thee (and) glory.
Letare.	Rejoice.
Luto gratulante.	Delighting in filth.
Lux fulgebit.	The Light shall shine.
Malorum.	Of the wicked.
Mane nobiscum, Domine.	Abide with us, O Lord.
Maria, ne timeas.	Mary, fear not.
Marya ventre concepit.	Mary conceived in her womb.
Mater dulcissima baba.	The sweetest mother kisses (?)
Mater gratiosa.	Gracious mother.
Mater honorata.	Revered mother.
Mater salutaris.	Healing mother.
Matris in gremio.	In His mother's lap.
Michi plausus oscula dada.	Clapping hands, give me kisses(?)
Mira plenitudine.	In marvellous abundance.
Mirabile misterium.	Wonderful mystery.

Miranda res.	Wonderful thing.
Miserere me (nobis).	Have mercy on me (us).
Misterium mirabile.	Wonderful mystery.
Motu fertur proprio.	He is borne by His own motion.
Munera portantes.	Bringing gifts.
Natus est de virgine.	He was born of a virgin.
Nec dare.	Nor give.
Ne mentem sompnus opprimat.	Let not sleep oppress the mind.
Nobis preparavit.	He has prepared for us.
Nomen Maria virginis.	The name of the virgin (is) Mary.
Non ex virili semine.	Not of man's seed.
Non poterit alligare.	He will not be able to bind.
Nova cantica.	New songs.
Nova, nova: Ave fit ex Eva.	Tidings, tidings: Out of *Eva* is made *Avé*.
Novus sol de virgine.	A new sun of a virgin.
Nowell.	Christmas. In Middle English often *tidings* as if from French *nouvelles;* but really from Latin *natalem=birthday*.
Nullus memoravit.	None has told.
Nunc gaudet ecclesia.	Now the Church rejoices.
Nunc gaudet Maria.	Now Mary rejoices.
O facies plena gracie.	O countenance full of grace.
O flos de Jesse virgula.	O Flower of the branch of Jesse.
O Jesu parvule.	O little Jesus.
O lux beata Trinitas.	O blessed light of the Trinity.
O martyr invictissime.	O martyr most unconquered.
Omnes de Saba venient.	All shall come from Sheba.
Omnes gentes plaudite.	All ye nations, rejoice.
Omnia fecisti.	Ye have done all things.
Optans celi gaudia.	Hoping for the joys of heaven.
O Puer optime.	O best of children.
Par amour.	For love's sake.
Parens et puella.	Mother and maiden.
Pares forma.	Equal in form.
Pergens ad celestia.	Attaining to heaven.

Per regis imperia.	Through the king's realms.
Poscente.	Entreating (it).
Potencia demonis.	By the devil's power.
Potente.	O powerful One.
Precantis.	Praying.
Proface.	Welcome.
Pro peccante homine.	For sinful man.
Prophetarum carmine.	By the word (*lit.* song) of the prophets.
Pro sua superbia.	For his pride.
Protomartyr Stephane.	O Stephen, first of the martyrs.
Psallite gaudentes.	Sing rejoicing.
Puer natus.	A Son is born.
Puer natus est nobis (nobis natus est).	Unto us a Son is born.
Que vocatur Maria.	Who is called Mary.
Quia lapidaverunt Stephanum.	Because they stoned Stephen.
Quia missus est angelus Gabriel.	Because the angel Gabriel is sent.
Quia Salvator mundi natus est.	Because the Saviour of the world is born.
Quia tecum est Dominus.	Because the Lord is with thee.
Quia virum non cognosco.	Because I know not a man.
Qui creavit omnia.	Who created all things.
Quid petis, O Fili?	What seekest Thou, O my Son?
Qui estis in convivio.	Ye who are at the feast.
Qui hodie natus es nobis.	Who is born to us on this day.
Qui natus est (es—second person) de virgine.	Who is born of a virgin.
Qui regnat super ethera.	Who reigns in heaven.
Qui triumphavit hodie.	Who triumphed to-day.
Quod Puer natus est nobis.	Because a Child is born to us.
Quot estis in convivio.	As many as are at this feast.
Reddens laudes Domino.	Giving thanks to the Lord.
Redemptoris mater.	Mother of the Redeemer.
Regem natum venerantes.	Worshipping the King that is born.
Reges de Saba venient.	Kings shall come from Sheba.
Regina celi, letare.	Queen of Heaven, rejoice.

Regnat Dei gracia.	The grace of God reigns.
Reluxit nobis hodie.	Has shone upon us to-day.
Repente.	Suddenly.
Res miranda.	Wonderful thing.
Rex pacificus.	The peacemaking King.
Rosa sine spina.	Rose without thorn.
Sacra fluenta potare.	To drink of the sacred fountains.
Salvator mundi, Domine.	Saviour of the world, Lord.
Salvator mundi natus est.	The Saviour of the world is born.
Salvatorem mundi.	Saviour of the world.
Salvator sine crimine.	The Saviour without sin.
Salve.	Hail.
Salve regina, mater misericordie.	Hail, queen, mother of pity.
Secreta que non noverat.	The secrets which she knew not.
Secundum verbum Tuum, fiat michi.	Let it be done to me according to Thy word.
Servire cantico.	To serve it with song.
Servite cum cantico.	Serve it with song.
Sicut voluisti.	As you have wished.
Sine contumelia.	Without disgrace.
Solamen miserorum.	Comfort of the wretched.
Sol de stella.	Sun of a star.
Spes eterne glorie.	Hope of eternal glory.
Stelle ducti lumine.	Guided by the light of the star.
Sua morte pia.	By His blessed death.
Sua morte propria.	By his own death.
Sua nocte pessima.	On his worst night.
Summi Largitor premii.	Dispenser of the supreme reward.
Summi Patris gracia.	By the grace of the Father Most High.
Tam gnare.	So wisely.
Te confitemur, Te eternum.	We acknowledge Thee as eternal.
Te Deum laudamus.	We praise Thee as God.
Te laudamus, Te Dominum.	We praise Thee as Lord.
Te Reformator sensuum.	Thee, renewer of the senses.
Teste prophecia.	By the witness of the prophets.

Trahe me post Te.	Draw me after Thee.
Transeamus.	Let us follow.
Trinitatis unitas.	The Oneness of the Trinity.
Tutrix orphanorum.	The guardian (fem.) of orphans.
Tuum precor Filium.	I pray to Thy Son.
Ubi sunt gaudia.	Where joys are.
Ullo sine crimine.	Without any sin.
Ut castytatis lyllyum.	As the lily of chastity.
Ut nos purget a crimine.	That He may cleanse us from sin.
Ut nova.	Lo, news.
Ut supra.	As above.
Velut maris stella.	Like a star of the sea.
Veni coronaberis.	Come, you shall be crowned.
Veni, Creator Spiritus.	Come, Creative Spirit.
Veni, Redemptor (omnium) gencium.	Come, Redeemer of (all) mankind.
Venter puelle baiulat.	A maiden's womb bears.
Ventre quem portasti.	Whom thou didst bear in thy womb.
Ventus de terra orta est.	A wind has arisen from the earth.
Verbo concepit Filium.	She conceived a Son by the Word.
Verbo prophesye.	In the word of prophecy.
Verbum caro factum est.	The Word is made flesh.
Verbum Patris hodie processit ex virgine.	The Word of the Father proceedeth this day from a virgin.
Verbum superum prodiens.	Showing forth the high Word.
Vere consolatrix.	Truly a consoler (fem.).
Vere nuncuparis.	You shall be called truly.
Veritas de terra orta est.	Truth is arisen of the earth.
Victore triumphante.	Victor triumphing.
Virgo gloriosa.	Glorious virgin.
Virgo rosa virginum.	A maiden, the rose of maidens.
Viri sine semine.	Without seed of man.
Volente.	Willing.
Vox clara ecce intonat.	Lo, a clear voice sounds.

INDEX TO FIRST LINES